Universität Würzburg

The Holy Scriptures in Ireland one thousand years ago

Selections from the Würzburg glosses

Universität Würzburg

The Holy Scriptures in Ireland one thousand years ago
Selections from the Würzburg glosses

ISBN/EAN: 9783337282271

Printed in Europe, USA, Canada, Australia, Japan

Cover: Foto ©Lupo / pixelio.de

More available books at **www.hansebooks.com**

THE
HOLY SCRIPTURES IN IRELAND
ONE THOUSAND YEARS AGO:

SELECTIONS
FROM
THE WÜRTZBURG GLOSSES.

TRANSLATED BY

REV. THOMAS OLDEN, A.B., M.R.I.A.,
VICAR OF BALLYCLOUGH.

DUBLIN:
HODGES, FIGGIS, AND CO., GRAFTON STREET,
PUBLISHERS TO THE UNIVERSITY.
LONDON: SIMPKIN, MARSHALL, AND CO.

1888.

PREFACE.

THE Commentary from which the following selections are taken is preserved in the University (formerly the Cathedral) library of Würtzburg, in Germany, where it has been from time immemorial. Nothing is known of the person by whom, or the time at which, it was brought there; but as Würtzburg was frequented by Irish ecclesiastics in the eleventh and twelfth centuries, and its monastery was of Irish foundation, there is little doubt that the manuscript was brought from Ireland by one of the many pilgrims who passed over to the Continent: and he happily placed it in the safe depository where it still remains. It contains a Latin version of St. Paul's Epistles, with Irish glosses or comments written between the lines of the text and round the margin, as shown in the facsimile. They terminate at Hebrews vii. 5. The manuscript has no date, but the language of the glosses is pronounced by competent authority[1] to be of the eighth or the beginning of the ninth century. How early this is may be judged from a few historical facts. Charlemagne was probably reigning at Aix-la-Chapelle, or at least he could not have been long in his grave; Alfred of England had not yet ascended the throne; two centuries or more had to elapse before the consummation of the great schism between the Churches of the East and West, and more than three before the Anglo-Norman conquest of Ireland.

[1] Zeuss, Grammatica Celtica, 2nd Ed. Berlin, MDCCCLXXI. Preface, p. xxiv. Referring to this and other MSS. of the same class, he says: "The language of all these manuscripts is the same, and they are to be assigned either to the eighth or the beginning of the ninth century."

The handwriting of three scribes is discernible in the glosses, though they are mainly the work of one. The names of all are unknown, and it can only be affirmed with certainty that the Commentary was written by Irishmen and for Irishmen, and is therefore a genuine relic of the ancient Church. It has a great advantage over many other ancient documents, in being free from the suspicion of interpolation or alteration; for when the Irish monasteries on the Continent lost their national character from the cessation of the stream of Irish pilgrims, there was no one who could read the language.

The existence of this precious manuscript was little known until the appearance of the great work of Zeuss on Celtic Grammar, in which it was largely quoted.

The whole of the glosses were afterwards published by Professor Zimmer,[1] and recently a new edition, with a literal translation, has been brought out by Mr. Whitley Stokes.[2]

Some time after the appearance of Zimmer's work, I made a translation of some parts of it; but not feeling satisfied with the result, I laid it aside.[3] Subsequently Mr. Stokes having asked me to read the proofs of his translation, I took up the subject again, and having revised my work with the aid of his exact literal version, I decided on carrying out my original intention of publishing it. So far, therefore, as accuracy is concerned, it is largely indebted to the work of that distinguished scholar. In making these selections, my object is to give a fair representation of the whole work in a moderate compass, with such illustrations from other sources as circumstances enable me to add. I could have wished that these were more numerous; but living at a distance from libraries, I am obliged to be content with calling public attention to the Commentary

---

[1] Glossæ Hibernicæ. Berlin. MDCCCLXXXI.

[2] The Old Irish Glosses of Würtzburg and Carlsruhe, by Whitley Stokes, D.C.L. Printed for the Philological Societies of London and Cambridge. Austin. Hertford, 1887.

[3] The difficulty of the language is very great, owing to its early date. In English, Chaucer cannot now be read without a glossary, and even then is difficult; but this is five centuries older than Chaucer.

by these selections, and must leave it to others who have leisure, and are within reach of books, to pursue the enquiry.

The following are the omissions which have been made:—

1. Most of the passages which are merely translations of the Latin text into Irish.

2. Repetitions of the same thought on parallel texts.

3. Places where the manuscript is partly illegible, or the sense has not been fully ascertained.

The glosses are so extremely concise, owing to the necessity of compression for want of space, that their full meaning is not always apparent at first sight, and it is possible that some passages of interest may have been omitted; but if this is so, they cannot be many, and the reader may feel assured that the general character of the whole is represented by the present work. Those who may desire to examine the entire Commentary will have no difficulty in doing so in Mr. Whitley Stokes' book,[1] where they will find the original and a literal translation.

Some Latin passages are intermingled with the Irish in the glosses. These are generally from authors whose names are given. Most of them are from Pelagius, the rest from Jerome, Augustine, Origen, Gregory the Great, and Isidore of Seville. Here the orthodox divines of the early Church, Augustine and Jerome, are found in company with Pelagius and Origen, who incurred the condemnation of Councils for errors of doctrine. Pelagius in particular was the most noted heresiarch of early times, and was strenuously opposed by both Jerome and Augustine. But though the compilers of the glosses draw their materials from many sources, they do not follow any author implicitly, but deal with all in an impartial spirit, treating their views on their merits without respect of persons. The source of the Irish notes which constitute the Commentary is not indicated in the manuscript, but some of these also are from Pelagius, others from Hilary and Primasius.[2] The writers were not, how-

---

[1] They may be forewarned, however, that the work is intended for philologists, and is not of a popular character.

[2] See Appendix, pp. 122-124.

ever, indifferent to errors of doctrine, as appears from their reference to heretics on two or three occasions. Thus at Romans v. 14 the Pelagians are so described; at 1 Thessalonians iv. 14 those holding the opinions known as Docetic, by which the reality of our Lord's body was denied; at 2 Timothy ii. 17, 18, those who denied the Resurrection. There appear also to be allusions to errors, as at Hebrews i. 5, where the heresy of the Adoptionists is probably referred to. The names of the heretics are never given, though they are found in the text of the commentator from whom the gloss is taken. It would seem that the atmosphere of Ireland was so serene,[1] theologically at least, that it was unnecessary to trouble the student with the names of those whose opinions had never reached their shores. For the same reason, perhaps, glosses are sometimes admitted without hesitation which do not take account of controversies carried on elsewhere, and might be interpreted in an unfavourable sense if employed at the present day. References to extinct discussions also occur, as, for instance, that on trine immersion in baptism, which is alluded to at Ephesians iv. 5 and Colossians ii. 12. A special interest attaches to this Commentary, as illustrating the teaching of those Irish schools of which Bede and others speak so highly, but of which so little is really known. At that period when, as Dr. Johnson has observed, Ireland was "the school of the West, the quiet habitation of sanctity and literature," she sent forth many eminent men, natives and foreigners, to do battle with heathenism on the Continent and in England; and the reputation of her schools, especially for the teaching of

---

[1] One of the few instances of a theological discussion between Irish divines is that recorded in the case of Colchu Lector of Clonmacnois (*d*. 792). The community had a difference with some eminent divines on a question of doctrine, and Colchu was appointed their representative. He had made St. Paul's Epistles a special study, and accepted him as "his master and patron in the letter as well as in the spirit." In the controversy which ensued this knowledge was of such advantage to him that his arguments prevailed. In consequence of his successful vindication of St. Paul, the story went that when returning, laden with books, from the assembly, St. Paul appeared in person, relieved him of his burthen, and bore it for him to his destination. Colchu was a correspondent of Alcuin's, then at the court of Charlemagne. See my article on Colchu in the *Dictionary of National Biography*.

the Holy Scriptures, stood very high throughout Western Europe. Archbishop Ussher has collected many testimonies from foreign writers on this subject, one of which may be given here as a specimen. It relates to the great school at Lismore, in the County of Waterford, which is said to have been attended by large numbers of foreigners, and it may be thus translated:—

> "Now haste Sicambri[1] from the marshy Rhine;
> Bohemians now desert their cold north land;
> Auvergne and Holland, too, add to the tide.
> Forth from Geneva's frowning cliffs they throng;
> Helvetia's youth by Rhone and by Saône
> Are few: the Western isle is now their home.
> All these from many lands, by many diverse paths,
> Rivals in pious zeal, seek Lismore's famous seat."[2]

The poet is eloquent and enthusiastic, but there must certainly have been some element of truth in this description of the students of Lismore.

The manner in which the Holy Scriptures were studied may be gathered from this Commentary. The students were not restricted to any special system of doctrine. On the contrary, they had opportunities of learning the views of the different schools of theology in the East as well as in the West. Thus on many passages two glosses are given representing different schools of interpretation, and sometimes as many as five are found, no suggestion being afforded as to which was to be preferred. The habit thus acquired of looking at a subject from different points of view, conduced to independence of thought, and helps to account for the difference which Mosheim and others notice between the Irish clergy abroad and their continental brethren in the ninth century. "The Irish doctors alone, and among them John Scotus, ventured to explain the doctrines of Christianity in a philosophical manner. But they generally

---

[1] The Sicambri occupied the country between the lower course of the Meuse and the Rhine.
[2] Bonaventure Moronus, in Ussher (Works), VI., 300.

incurred strong disapprobation: for the Latin theologians in that age would allow no place for philosophy in matters of religion."[1] To the same purport are Mr. Haddan's words: "The difference between Ireland and other parts of the Church lay chiefly in her possessing a wider and more self-grown learning, and in the consequent boldness and independence of her speculations."[2]

The reader will not expect to find any new light thrown on the interpretation of Scripture, for the sources from which the glosses are drawn have long been known and used by scholars; but he cannot fail to be interested in finding so intelligent a Commentary produced in Ireland at this early period. It is the earliest[3] Commentary on St. Paul's Epistles in the British Islands, and is, therefore, an original compilation. The authors were undoubtedly men of learning, and they had read as widely as circumstances permitted. They were also men of sincere piety, as one may judge from the ejaculations which occur now and then—the expressions of the author's feelings as he meditates on the great truths he is treating of. Thus at Romans viii. 17, when the words "joint-heirs with Christ" come before him, he exclaims, "Oh, the inheritance with Christ!" Again, at 2 Thessalonians i. 6, full of sympathy for the trials of that Church, he cries out, "O ye righteous ones!"

It has already been mentioned that the glosses are on the Latin translation of the Epistles. This sometimes agrees in sense with the Authorized English translation, at other times with the Revised or the Rhemish, and occasionally it differs from all three. As therefore no English translation exactly corresponded with it, it seemed most convenient to give the Authorized Version in the portion of the text which accompanies the glosses, placing the various readings, when necessary, at the foot of the page.

---

[1] Mosheim (Soames' Ed.), II., 225.
[2] Remains of Rev. A. W. Haddan, p. 293.
[3] We have nothing of Bede's on St. Paul's Epistles, and Alcuin only wrote on Titus, Philemon, and Hebrews.

Preface. xi

Some remarks on the sources of Irish theology, which may not interest the general reader, have been added as an Appendix.

The passages from Latin commentators, quoted in the notes, are given in the original, for the information of those who may wish to know the sources of the glosses to which they refer. It has not been thought necessary to translate them, as the glosses are the translations, being sometimes taken word for word from them.

It only remains for me to express my thanks to the Rev. Dr. Salmon, Provost of Trinity College; to Rev. Dr. Gwynn, Regius Professor of Divinity; to Rev. H. E. White, Chaplain to the Bishop of Salisbury, and many other friends, for kind assistance; also to Professor Zimmer, for permitting his facsimile of a portion of the manuscript to be reproduced for this work.

ABBREVIATIONS.

A.V.—Authorized Version.
R.V.—Revised Version.
Rh.V.—Rhemish Version.

WÜRTZBURG GLOSSES.

ROMANS.

CHAP. I.

8. First, I thank my God through Jesus Christ for you all, that your faith is spoken of throughout the whole world.

my God—[that is] in a general sense, for He is the God of everyone in the primal creation:

or, in a special sense, because He bestowed on him (St. Paul) the Holy Spirit and the grace of preaching.

through Jesus Christ.—Further, He is "my God,"[1] because I believe in Jesus Christ, [and] as He Himself has said, "No man cometh to the Father but by me." (John xiv. 6.)

your faith.—It is well known in every land that you have become believers in God, and great is the advantage of it to us; for since the chief rulers of the world have become believers, everyone will follow their example, and whosoever shall believe need not fear persecution.[2]

9. For God is my witness, whom I serve with my spirit in the Gospel of his Son, that without ceasing I make mention of you always in my prayers.

witness.—He knows: there is no concealment from Him.

without intermission.—There are two things which He does not, viz.: to intermit making mention of them, or to intermit praying for them.

---

8. [1] Natura Deus omnium: merito et voluntate paucorum est, ideo dixit, "Deo meo." (Pelagius and Primasius.)

8. [2] Qui non crediderant poterant credere horum exemplo. Facile enim facit inferior quod fieri viderit a priore. (Hilary.)

11. For I long to see you, that I may impart unto you some spiritual gift, to the end ye may be established.

   to see you.—What is it brings me to you? The answer is not difficult; it is, that I long to see you.

   some spiritual gift.—It is not the full gift of the Spirit he speaks of here, for they had received a portion of Divine grace before. Let me now, he says, supply what is needed to make your faith perfect.

12. That I may be comforted together with you by the mutual faith both of you and me.

   comforted—so that the perfection of your faith may be a comfort to me.

13. That I might have some fruit among you also, even as among other Gentiles.

   fruit.—That he might have the fruit of his ministry with God; for the gaining of a multitude of believers through his preaching secures a good reward to him.

14. I am debtor both to the Greeks, and to the Barbarians; both to the wise and to the unwise.

   Greeks.—That is, all the wise nations.[1]

   Barbarians.—That is, the foreigners.[2]

   debtor.—It is my duty to preach to all, for I speak in the tongues of all [Acts ii. 8]. I am a debtor to all, both the wise and unwise.

16. For I am not ashamed of the Gospel of Christ: for it is the power of God unto salvation to every one that believeth; to the Jew first, and also to the Greek.

   Gospel.—I am not ashamed of the preaching of the Gospel; that is, the preaching of the Passion and Incarnation[3] of Christ, because the miracles of His resurrection and ascension follow.[4]

---

14. [1] Sapientes Græcos philosophos, Barbaros insipientes appellat. (Pelagius.)

14. [2] Foreign, *i.e.*, external to the Roman Empire, of which St. Paul was a citizen.

16. [3] This inverted order of events occurs frequently.

16. [4] Contra eos qui negant Christum in carne et erubescunt nativitatem Domini et crucem: qui putant hæc indigna Deo non intelligentes nihil dignius Deo quam quod ad humanam salutem proficit. (Pelagius and Primasius.)

Greek.—He says, "Go ye and teach all nations" (Matt. xxviii. 19); [so] the Jews have the pre-eminence in race, but not in faith.

19. That which may be known of God is manifest in them; for God hath shewed it unto them.

   shewed it—that is, the knowledge and worship of God; because they cannot but serve Him.

20. For the invisible things of him from the creation of the world are clearly seen, being understood by the things that are made, even his eternal power and Godhead; so that they are without excuse.

    understood.—It is manifest to them that [the universe] is the work of an excellent[1] Being.
    clearly seen.—By the elements His eternity is seen.

21. They glorified him not as God, neither were thankful; but became vain in their imaginations, and their foolish heart was darkened.

    as God.—They shewed none of the reverence due to God.
    darkened.—As they receded from the light of truth (Pelagius), that is, from the light of the knowledge of God.

23. And changed the glory of the incorruptible God into an image made like[2] to corruptible man.

    image (or *likeness of an image*).—It was not an image they adored, but the likeness of an image.

24. To dishonour their own bodies between themselves.

    between themselves.—That is, when in their idolatrous rites they inflict burnings and brandings on themselves. (Pelagius.)

---

20. [1] Literally "an ordained Being:" *fir oirdnithi.*
23. [2] "The likeness of an image of."—R.V.
24. [3] Primasius has this in a somewhat different wording: "Dum sibi caracteres et ustiones infligunt in consecrationibus idolorum."

26. For this cause God gave them up unto vile affections.

this cause—for the above-mentioned cause; that is, because they served the creature, not the Creator.

CHAP. II.

1. Therefore thou art inexcusable, O man,[1] whosoever thou art that judgest: for wherein thou judgest another, thou condemnest thyself; for thou that judgest doest the same things.

O man.—O all man[kind]; or, O every man.

doest—that is, in will; when thou consentest to them. It is manifest that thou art a bad man, when thou judgest and blamest the evil to which thou consentest.

2. For we are sure that the judgment of God is according to truth against them which commit such things.

according to truth—[the person] was not to be connived at, but left to a just judge.

3. Thinkest thou this, O man?

thinkest—thou thinkest; or it may be interrogative (thinkest thou?)

4. Not knowing that the goodness of God leadeth thee to repentance.

leadeth thee.—He bestows every good thing on thee, to lead thy mind to the knowledge of Him.

7. To them who by patient continuance in well-doing seek for glory and honour and immortality, eternal life.

glory.—Because "the saints shall shine forth as the sun"[2] (Matt. xiii. 43). (Pelagius.)

honour.—The honour of the sons of God, whereby they shall judge the fugitive angels (1 Cor. vi. 3; Jude 6). (Pelagius.)

eternal life.—Those who endure all trials in the present life, and are advancing to glory and honour in the future.

II. 1. [1] O homo omnis.

7. [2] Gloriam illam prædicat qua sancti fulgebunt ut sol. Honorem filiorum Dei, quid enim honoratius filiis Dei qui etiam angelos judicabunt. It will be observed that Primasius in taking this passage from Pelagius omits the word "*fugitivos.*"

11. For there is no respect of persons with God.

> *persons.*—He accepts not persons, but works: that is, it is no defence for anyone to say, "the law did not come to us" (Gentiles).

12. For as many as have sinned without law shall also perish without law; and as many as have sinned in the law shall be judged by the law.

> *without law.*—As there was no moderation (or restraint of law) in their sin, so there shall be none in their punishment.

13. For not the hearers of the law are just before God, but the doers of the law shall be justified.

> *hearers.*—They will perish through the law that they have outraged.

15. Their thoughts meanwhile accusing or else excusing one another.

> *thoughts.*—They meditate on what good there is to be done, and encourage its performance, but they condemn and forbid what is evil.

16. In the day when God shall judge the secrets of men by Jesus Christ according to my Gospel.[1]

> *by Jesus Christ.*—That is, it is through Jesus I preach:
>> or, (2) God the Father shall execute judgment by Jesus Christ;[2] that is, the Son shall judge in the day of judgment, according to our Lord's words: "He hath committed all judgment to the Son." (John v. 22.)

---

16. [1] According to my Gospel by Jesus Christ.—R.V.
16. [2] Secundum quod annuncio per Jesum Christum: sive per Jesum Christum judicabit Deus occulta hominum. (Primasius.)
Primasius took the first part of this note from Pelagius.

23. Thou that makest thy boast of the law, by breaking the law dishonourest thou God?

> *breaking the law.*—Thou sayest thou art happy because thou knowest the will of God, while thou passest by the sense of the Law relating to the Incarnation of Christ, and thus thou dishonourest God (Pelagius):[1] or, (2), Because thou believest not in Christ whom the Law preaches.

25. For circumcision verily profiteth, if thou keep the law; but if thou be a breaker of the law, thy circumcision is made uncircumcision.

> *profiteth.*—Circumcision protects from the condemnation of the Law, for with them (the Jews) he who was not circumcised was guilty of death.
>
> *keep the law.*—That is, the mystery[2] of the Law; as it is said, "the Law prophesied Christ."[3] (Matt. xi. 13.)

27. Shall not uncircumcision which is by nature, if it fulfil the law, judge thee, who by the letter and circumcision dost transgress the law?

> *judge thee.*—He will surpass thee, O Jew; that is, he will be better than thou art.

CHAP. III.

1. What advantage then hath the Jew? or what profit is there of circumcision?

> *what advantage.*—If those who are uncircumcised are so favourably situated, what is the advantage of circumcision? In reply, he proceeds, not to declare the benefit of circumcision, but to praise the Jews.

---

23. [1] This gloss, erroneously attributed to Pelagius in the MS., is found in the earlier Commentary of Hilary the Deacon: "Prævaricator legis es quando sensum legis qui de incarnatione et divinitate Christi est præteris: et Deum inhonoras dum testimonium ejus quod dedit de filio suo non recipis: ipse enim dixit hic est filius meus dilectus."

So Origen: "Salvator in evangeliis dicit quia Moyses de me scripsit : Qui ergo non credit Christo de quo Moyses scripsit in lege destruit legem; qui autem credit Christo de quo Moyses scripsit, legem confirmat per fidem qua credit in Christum."

25. [2] The figurative or mystical interpretation of the Scriptures is one of the characteristics of this Commentary.

25. [3] Si lex servetur, id est si in Christum credatur qui promissus est Abrahæ. Hic servat legem qui credit in Christo. (Hilary.)

2. Much every way: chiefly, because that unto them were committed the oracles of God.

> *much.*—Greatly is the Jew better than the Gentile; this is an answer to the Gentile given on behalf of the Jew.

8. And not rather (as we be slanderously reported, and as some affirm that we say), Let us do evil, that good may come? whose damnation is just.

> *affirm that we say.*—Is it not as if we were slandered? It is like it; nay, it is so. They accuse us of saying it; as Paul has said [are their words] " Where sin abounded, grace did much more abound." (Rom. v. 20.)

9. What then? are we better than they? No, in no wise: for we have before proved both Jews and Gentiles, that they are all under sin.

> *better.*—We do not differ the one from the other; we are all guilty.
> *Jews and Gentiles.*—All the nations.

11. There is none that understandeth, there is none that seeketh after God.

> *understandeth.*—The want of knowledge is a cause of unrighteousness; and the reason one is without knowledge and righteousness is that he has not sought after [Him].[1]

12. They are all gone out of the way, they are together become unprofitable; there is none that doeth good, no, not one.[2]

> *out of the way.*—Because they sought not after God.
> *all.*—Without exception.
> *not one.*—Even until the One, that is even until Christ;[3] for He found not anything good before Him in the world.

---

11. [1] Qui non intelligit non requirit, seu ideo non intelligit quia non quærit. (Primasius.)
12. [2] The Latin is, "*usque ad unum*," which the Commentator translates "until the One."
12. [3] Quidam dicunt, usque ad Christum. (Primasius.)

19. That every mouth may be stopped, and all the world may become guilty before God.

stopped.—So that no one should boast that his merit saved him.

22. Even the righteousness of God which is by faith of Jesus Christ unto[1] all and upon[2] all them that believe; for there is no difference.

righteousness of God.—Into the bodies and souls of sinners.

Jesus Christ.—It is through faith in Jesus Christ everyone becomes righteous.

upon all.—He is over them at a height which is not realized.

24. Being justified freely by his grace through the redemption that is in Christ Jesus.

justified.—By faith only; that is, by the faith of belief in Jesus Christ. It is He that redeemed us, and He is then our ransom through His blood.

25. Whom God hath set forth[3] to be a propitiation through faith in his blood, to declare his righteousness for the remission of sins that are past, through the forbearance of God.

set forth (or *purposed*).—It was purposed in the secret counsels of the Deity that He should be the propitiation for them that believe, that they might be set free by His blood.

through faith.—Through the faith of everyone who believes in his salvation through His blood.

29. Is he the God of the Jews only? is he not also of the Gentiles? Yes, of the Gentiles also.

of the Jews.—Did He create them alone? did He not create all men?[4] Here is a reply to the thoughts of the Jews.

of the Gentiles.—He is [even] nearer to the Gentiles, because before the Law there were saints who pleased God, as Abel, Seth, Enoch, Noah.[5]

---

22. [1] "*In omnes*," which may mean "into all." [2] "*Super omnes*," which is taken to mean "over all."

25. [3] Purposed.—R.V. margin.

29. [4] Numquid Judæos solos Deus creavit: aut de illis solis curam gerit. (Pelagius.)

29. [5] Id est multo magis et gentium quia ante legem sancti Deo placuerunt, sicut Abel, Noe, et cæteri. (Primasius.)

31. Do we make void the law through faith? God forbid: yea, we establish the law.

void.—Do we destroy the Law when we say through faith?

we establish.—[we do so] While we prove the truth of God's promise, "A new heart also will I give you, and a new spirit will I put within you; and I will take away the stony heart out of your flesh, and I will give to you a heart of flesh" (Ezekiel xxxvi. 26); that is, that after the stony[1] there should be a spiritual circumcision.

CHAP. IV.

1. What shall we say then that Abraham our father, as pertaining to the flesh, hath found?

our father.—That is, according to the circumcision of the flesh :[2] or, he is our father "according to the flesh," because they (the Jews) were of the race of Abraham.

4. Now to him that worketh is the reward not reckoned of grace, but of debt.

grace.—If this is payment, it is not of grace but of debt. It was through grace, then, he was sanctified, and not for the fulfilling of the Law.

5. But to him that worketh not, but believeth on him that justifieth the ungodly, his faith is counted for righteousness.

faith.—He is to be justified by faith.

12. The father of circumcision to them who are not of the circumcision only, but who also walk in the steps of that faith of our father Abraham, which he had being yet uncircumcised.

circumcision only.—Not to those who undergo fleshly circumcision only, if they do not accomplish the mystical circumcision of their vices.

father Abraham.—He is the father of those who have perfect faith as he had.

---

31. [1] The glosser refers to the flint knives with which circumcision was performed. See Exodus iv. 25; Joshua v. 3. (Wh. Stokes.)
1. [2] Patrem secundum carnis circumcisionem. (Pelagius and Primasius.)

11. And he received the sign of circumcision, a seal of the righteousness of the faith which he had yet being uncircumcised.

   sign.—That there might be in his body that which would signify the cutting off of vices from his soul.

   seal.—This is a repetition with regard to the sign; was he circumcised when he was justified by faith?

13. For the promise, that he should be the heir of the world, was not to Abraham, or to his seed, through the law, but through the righteousness of faith.

   seed.—It was foretold then that his children should be illustrious; as it is said, "In thy seed shall all the nations of the earth be blessed." (Gen. xxii. 18).

   righteousness of faith.—It is through its faith it (the seed) has every good thing.

14. For if they which are of the law be heirs, faith is made void, and the promise made of none effect.

   heirs.—The Jews, the children of Abraham.

   of none effect.—Abolished is the promise to Abraham, "I have made thee a father of many nations." (Gen. xvii. 5.)

15. Because the law worketh wrath: for where no law is there is no transgression.

   worketh wrath.—The grace of pardon would not have been obtained, nor the promise, if it had been given through the Law; for unless this is fulfilled, vengeance! vengeance! has its course.

16. Therefore it is of faith, that it might be by grace; to the end the promise might be sure to all the seed.

   promise.—The inheritances which Abraham obtained were two in number: a carnal inheritance by circumcision, viz., the promised land, and that was what Isaac received; and a spiritual inheritance by faith, and thereby he is the father of many nations.

17. As it is written, I have made thee a father of many nations.

nations.—Not of the nation of Israel only, but of all the faithful in the world. (Pelagius.)

24. For us also, to whom it shall be imputed, if we believe on him that raised up Jesus our Lord from the dead.

imputed.—That which was reckoned unto Abraham, that is, righteousness through faith.

25. Who was delivered for our offences, and was raised again for our justification.

our justification.—He speaks in the person of the believer, that he might confirm the righteousness of the believer. It is evident to us by His resurrection that He is true God. (Chap. i. 4.)

CHAP. V.

6. When we were yet without strength, in due time Christ died for the ungodly.

ungodly.—All were ungodly, as [it is written] "There is none that doeth good, no, not one." (Chap. iii. 12.)

8. But God commendeth his love toward us, in that while we were yet sinners Christ died for us.

love.—He commends; that is, He deserves to be loved by us, while He dared what no other did. For when anything is given that is not due, charity is most highly commended.[1] . . So that they may understand what their conduct should be.

9. Much more then, being now justified by his blood, we shall be saved from wrath through him.

saved.—Since He has saved us from our sins, so that we are justified from them, much more will He save us from the wrath to come.

---

8. [1] This gloss is composed of portions of two comments from Pelagius, which are as follows:—[Quando enim indebite aliquid præstatur tunc maxime caritas commendatur]. Quid enim tam indebite quam ut sine peccato Dominus pro servis impiis moreretur, &c.

Notandum quod plerumque Apostolus credentes jam in Christo fuisse peccatores dicens jam non esse significat [ut qualiter se exhibere debeant recognoscant].

11. And not only so, but we also joy in God through our Lord Jesus Christ, by whom we have now received the atonement.¹

> *atonement* (or *reconciliation*).—That is, peace with God through faith in Christ.

13. For until the law sin was in the world; but sin is not imputed when there is no law.

> *in the world.*—Without men being warned of it, or perceiving it.
> *no law.*—For there was no knowledge [of it] till the Law came; for sin had the human race under its dominion.

14. Death reigned from Adam to Moses, even over them that had not sinned after the similitude of Adam's transgression, who is the figure of him that was to come.

> *Adam's transgression.*—Though I say it was not imputed.

15. But not as the offence, so also is the free gift. For if through the offence of one many be dead, much more the grace of God, and the gift by grace, which is by one man, Jesus Christ, hath abounded unto many.

> *offence.*—This is an answer to the opinions of the heretics who say: if the sin of Adam harmed those who were not sinners, then the righteousness of Christ benefits those who are not believers.²

16. And not as it was by one³ that sinned, so is the gift: for the judgment was by one to condemnation, but the free gift is of many offences unto justification.

> *one* (or *one sin*).—Judgment is through one sin by Adam; grace of many offences, by Jesus Christ, unto men.

---

11. ¹ Reconciliation.—R.V.

15. ² The heretics here referred to are the Pelagians. The passage quoted is not now found in Pelagius' Commentary, but St. Augustine quotes and replies to it in one of his letters (Migne xliv. col. 186.)

He explains Pelagius' argument thus. As it is impossible that Christ's righteousness can confer any benefit on unbelievers, it follows that infants are not affected by Adam's sin. Absurdissimum utique et falsissimum judicant ut Christi justitia etiam non credentibus prosit unde putant confici nec primi hominis peccatum parvulis non peccantibus nocere potuisse, sicut et Christi justitia prodesse ullis non credentibus non potest.

16. ³ One sin (Rhemish V.); also Whitby.

20. Moreover the law entered, that the offence might abound. But where sin abounded, grace did much more abound.

sin abounded.—That is, when it was completely established, being manifested by the Law; then came the grace of Jesus Christ; because "the Law made no one[1] perfect." (Hebrews vii. 19.) This was not imputed before; it is manifest before all now.

21. That as sin hath reigned unto death, even so might grace reign through righteousness unto eternal life by Jesus Christ our Lord.

unto death—unto bodily and penal death.
Jesus Christ.—Through Him are grace, and truth, and life eternal.

CHAP. VI.

3. [Brethren][2] know ye not that so many of us as were baptized into Jesus Christ were baptized into his death?

brethren.—O Jews and O faithful Gentiles!
baptized.—That is, after the likeness of His death in the mortal body, from which He parted in His passion. He does not return to that body, but is now in a spiritual resurrection body, without expectation of death or decay. Let us therefore not return[3] to the mortal body of sin. [It is a body] for as our bodies are composed of members,[4] so sin is composed of vices.

4. Therefore we are buried with him by baptism into death; that like as Christ was raised up from the dead by the glory of the Father, even so we also should walk in newness of life.

baptism.—When we pass under baptism, it is the likeness of His burial and death to us.

---

20. [1] "*Neminem.*" The Vulgate reads "*nihil*" (nothing), agreeing with the A. V.

VI. 3. [2] *Fratres.* Not in Vulgate, A.V., R.V., or Rhemish.

3. [3] "Ad mortis Christi nos similitudinem suaderet mori debere peccato et consepeleri Christo."—ORIGEN on Romans vi.

3. [4] See Coloss. iii. 5, note. Also the following on verse 6—"That the body of sin might be destroyed"—Hoc est ut omnia vitia destruantur quia unum vitium membrum est peccati, omnia corpus totum. (Pelagius.)

Primasius follows this as far as "peccati," and then goes on: "Corpus vero universitas delictorum quorum principium *originale peccatum.*"

10. For in that[1] he died, he died unto sin once: but in that he liveth, he liveth unto God.

> *In that He died* (or, *He that is dead*).—Is once [for all] free from sin, as once Christ's flesh died.
>
> *liveth unto God.*—Christ's body is immortal, after the resurrection in the glory of the Deity.

11. Likewise reckon ye also yourselves to be dead indeed unto sin, but alive unto God through Jesus Christ our Lord.

> *alive.*—Be ye ever living in Jesus Christ, for ye are members of Him, for He "ever liveth." (Heb. vii. 25.)

12. Let not sin therefore reign in your mortal body, that ye should obey it in the lusts thereof.

> *lusts.*—This is what he means when he preaches, "We who are dead to sin, how shall we live therein again?"[2]
>
> *reign.*—That is in your mortal wills,[3] which procure death to you.

13. Neither yield ye your members as instruments of unrighteousness unto sin.

> *neither yield ye.*—Exhibit not your members in conflict before the devil.[4]

17. But God be thanked, that ye were the servants of sin, but ye have obeyed from the heart that form of doctrine which was delivered you.

> *servants.*—Whatever[5] nation it was to whom this Epistle was written, it is shown to have been under a yoke, for he says "Ye were the servants," &c.

---

10. [1] "Qui enim mortuus est." The Vulgate has "quod," agreeing with A.V.
12. [2] "Iterum." The Vulgate has "adhuc."
12. [3] Quomodo regnet peccatum in corpore exposuit, per obedientiam scilicet et consensum. (Pelagius.)
13. [4] Ostendit Diabolum nostris nos jaculis impugnare occasio enim datur illi per nostra peccata. (Primasius.)
17. [5] This implies that the writer did not know that the Epistle was addressed to the Romans. The gloss was therefore probably taken from some manuscript which was anonymous. According to Archdeacon Farrar, an important manuscript (the *Codex Boernerianus*, written in the Irish Monastery of St. Gall), omits the word "Rome" in chap. i. vv. 7, 15; and it has been inferred that the main body of the Epistle was sent to different churches with different terminations. Bishop Lightfoot thinks St. Paul circulated it in one form, without the two last chapters.—Farrar's "Messages of the Books," p. 291.

18. Being then made free from sin, ye became the servants of righteousness.

free.—Not through yourselves, but by God and His grace.

23. For the wages of sin is death; but the gift of God is eternal life through Jesus[1] Christ our Lord.

wages.—*Stipendium* is the name of the pay given to soldiers for military service.

through (or *in*) *Jesus Christ.*—Through faith in Jesus:
or (2), in the life wherein Jesus is after His resurrection.

CHAP. VII.

6. But now we are delivered from the law, that being dead wherein we were held; that we should serve in newness of spirit, and not in the oldness of the letter.

dead.—We are in a new position, for the sin we served hitherto is no longer alive. It was that which procured death to us.

newness of spirit.—In a new covenant after confession of faith [and] without sin.

7. What shall we say then? Is the law sin? God forbid. Nay, I had not known sin, but by the law: for I had not known lust, except the law had said, Thou shalt not covet.

law.—It is called "the law of sin" (ch. viii. 2), because it makes sins manifest. Pelagius says, that speaking in the person of one living under the Law, he says, " I did not perceive it to be sin."

lust.—Now I know concupiscence is sin, because it is forbidden.

8. But sin, taking occasion by the commandment, wrought in me all manner of concupiscence. For without the law sin was dead.

concupiscence.—It is sin which wrought all concupiscence; that is, any concupiscence which was forbidden by the Law was wrought in me by sin, and thereby the command of the law has been violated.

was dead.—I thought it was dead, because I perceived it not.

---

23. [1] In Christ Jesus.—R.V.

9. For I was alive without the law once: but when the commandment came, sin revived, and I died.

alive.—I thought I was alive when I did not perceive sin, until the Law came.

10. The commandment, which was ordained to life, I found to be unto death.

to life.—It would have been life to me if I fulfilled it.

11. For sin, taking occasion by the commandment, deceived me, and by it slew me.

deceived me.—I do it after it was prohibited by the commandment, "Thou shalt not covet."[1] (Verse 7.)

12. Wherefore the law is holy, and the commandment holy, and just, and good.

holy.—This is his decision, and a reply to what was said, "What shall we say then?" (Verse 7.)

13. Was then that which is good made death unto me? God forbid. But sin, that it might appear sin, working death in me by that which is good; that sin by the commandment might become exceeding sinful.

exceeding sinful.—It is more sinful after being perceived than before.

14. For we know that the law is spiritual: but I am carnal, sold under sin.

carnal.—Since Adam went contrary to God's will, I have habitually lived after the flesh. (Pelagius.)

sold.[2]—That is, by Adam; or, (2) my carnal will sold me so that I am under bondage to sin.

---

11. [1] Lust.—R. V. margin.
14. [2] St. Augustine has three interpretations, two of which are given in the gloss:—

Et hoc ex culpa primi hominis, qui pro delectatione cibi vetiti se et omnes alios, vendidit: vel sub peccato id est servi peccati sint: vel unusquisque vendidit se consuetudine propriæ voluntatis.

It will be observed that the first meaning in the gloss is inconsistent with the gloss on chap. v. 14, owing probably to their having been taken from different sources.

15. For that which I do I allow[1] not: for what I would, that I do not; but what I hate, that I do.
I do.—From my fleshly desires.

18. For I know that in me (that is, in my flesh) dwelleth no good thing: for to will is present with me; but how to perform that which is good I find not.
flesh.—It is not the flesh he blames, but the desires.
will.—It does not abide constantly with me, but is somewhat near me.
perform.—By this he means the carrying out of a good intention, without the interposition of a bad one.

22. For I delight in the law of God after the inward man.
delight.—This, therefore, is a proof that the law is good, of the discovery of which he speaks above.
inward man.—It is the soul that is ready to fulfil the law of God, and not the body.

24. O wretched man that I am! who shall deliver me from
25. the body of this death? I thank God[2] through Jesus Christ our Lord.
deliver me.—[No power] if the grace of God does not aid me; but it will, however.

CHAP. VIII.

1. There is therefore no condemnation to them which are in Christ Jesus, who walk not after the flesh, but after the Spirit.
no condemnation.—Here or yonder (*i.e.*, beyond the grave).
are in Christ Jesus.—Those who believe in Jesus.

2. For the law of the Spirit of life in Christ Jesus hath made me free from the law of sin and death.
law of the Spirit.—The spiritual law which procures life to us through faith in Jesus Christ.
law of sin.—The law of the Spirit hath saved me from the law of sin.
law of death.—The law of Moses; it was by him sin was made manifest, through which came death.

---

15. [1] I know. not.—R.V.
25. [2] Gratia Dei, the grace of God.—Rh. V.

3. For what the law could not do, in that it was weak through the flesh.

could not do—[could not] completely accomplish that justification.

4. That the righteousness[1] of the law might be fulfilled in us, who walk not after the flesh, but after the Spirit.

righteousness.—Some justification (or justifying power) there was in the Law.

after the Spirit.—Thus shall we be holy.

5. For they that are after the flesh do mind the things of the flesh.

after the flesh.—Out of such material it is not easy to make a saint.

6. For to be carnally minded[2] is death; but to be spiritually minded is life and peace.

carnally minded.—To return evil for evil. This, therefore, is "the prudence of the flesh,"[3] to have the thoughts wholly occupied with worldly cares, without any thought of heavenly things.

7. Because the carnal mind is enmity against God: for it is not subject to the law of God, neither indeed can be.

subject.—It is already burthened with care—that is, with thoughts about earthly things.

9. But ye are not in the flesh, but in the Spirit, if so be that the Spirit of God dwell in you.

ye.—Romans.

not in the flesh.—According to the custom of all good preachers, he praises and speaks gently to them before finding fault.

if the Spirit.—It is thus ye are, viz., in the Spirit, and it is easy for you to do good.

---

4. [1] Ordinance.—R.V.; Justification.—Rh. V.
6. [2] φρόνημα σαρκός. The mind of the flesh.—R.V. The wisdom of the flesh.—Rh. V.
6. [3] Prudentia carnis est ut unusquisque velit se vindicare: prudentia vero Spiritus non reddere malum pro malo. (Primasius.)

10. And if Christ be in you, the body is dead because of sin; but the Spirit is life because of righteousness.

> *in you.*—Though Christ be in you through confession of faith in baptism, and the soul is alive thereby, yet the body is dead through the old sins, and, though it has been cleansed through baptism, it is unable to do good works until the Holy Spirit awakes it.
>
> *dead.*—So that it does not commit sin.[1]

11. Shall quicken your mortal bodies by his Spirit that dwelleth in you.

> *mortal bodies.*—For that guest-house of the Spirit is not ignoble.

12. We are debtors, not to the flesh, to live after the flesh.

> *debtors.*—They are not sins of the flesh which are paid[2] for there now, whatever they may have been before.
>
> *to live after the flesh.*—To do the deeds after the flesh as formerly; though you are free, you owe debts, as we all do [he adds], to smooth over the subject of payment.

13. For if ye live after the flesh, ye shall die: but if ye through the Spirit do mortify the deeds of the body, ye shall live.

> *die.*—The penal death:[3] or [it means] bodily death.
>
> *mortify.*—Killing them, then, was not to be regretted.
>
> *live.*—An eternal life. There shall be life eternal if the deeds of the flesh are mortified.

---

10. [1] That is, sin has no more power to excite evil passions and desires in it. Spiritus vivit et vivificat ut justitiam faciamus: caro autem mortua est ne ab ea vincamur. (Primasius.)

[2] The "taxes of our flesh" was one of the expressions for sins among the ancient Irish.

13. [3] The usual expression for future punishment in this Commentary. The language is that of Pelagius, whose words are: "Significat autem mortem æternæ pœnæ." He held that the death of the body was not the penalty for sin. The second interpretation, which is therefore opposed to his views, is taken from some other source. In the gloss on chap. v. 14, both are combined.

14. For as many as are led by the Spirit of God, they are the sons of God.
> *led.*—Are driven; that is, if He is our pilot, as it is said of the Son, "He was led by the Spirit." (Matthew iv. 1.)

17. And if children, then heirs; heirs of God, and joint-heirs with Christ; if so be that we suffer with him, that we may be also glorified together.
> *heirs.*—Oh, the inheritance with Christ!
> *joint-heirs.*—We shall be like Him, that we may share [His glory]. We shall be joint-heirs if we suffer together like Christ, or with Christ, or with each other.
> *glorified.*—That the glory which was given to Christ may be given to us with Him, as it is said, "We know that when he shall appear we shall be like him." (1 John iii. 2).

19. The earnest expectation of the creature waiteth for the manifestation of the sons of God.
> *earnest.*—Such was the nature of its expectation.

20. For the creature was made subject to vanity, not willingly.
> *not willingly.*—It may have been necessary.[1]

26. Likewise the Spirit also helpeth our infirmities; for we know not what we should pray for as we ought; but the Spirit itself maketh intercession for us with groanings which cannot be uttered.
> *helpeth.*—It is thus the Spirit helps our weakness, when we have a common desire in body, soul, and spirit.[2] Then there is true prayer, but we cannot offer it without the inspiration of the Spirit. Our prayer is ineffectual if we ask only for present things, for in this the Spirit does not help us; but if we pray for glory in body and soul after the resurrection, we shall be helped by the Spirit.

---

20. [1] Literally, "unless it be necessary."
26. [2] See 1 Thessalonians v. 23.

27. And he that searcheth the hearts knoweth what is the mind[1] of the Spirit, because he maketh intercession for the saints according to the will of God.

>   *mind* (or *desires*) *of the Spirit.*—He says "the desires of the Spirit," because it is He who inspires those desires in man.
>
>   *will of God.*—Whatever God desires they should pray for, that He inspires in [the hearts of] His saints.

28. We know that all things work together for good to them that love God, to them who are the called according to his purpose.

>   *all things work.*—Whatsoever we shall have done for the love of God, whether it has prospered or failed, shall be followed by future glory.

29. For whom he did foreknow, he also did predestinate to be conformed to the image of his Son, that he might be the firstborn among many brethren.

>   *firstborn.*—The "firstborn from the dead," Coloss. i. 18 (as Pelagius says); that is, He is the firstborn of the faithful in His resurrection and [also] in the reception of glory. (1 Pet. i. 21.)

31. What shall we then say to these things? If God be for us, who can be against us?

>   *say.*—We should love Him who bestowed such benefits upon us (1 John iv. 19).
>
>   *for us.*—Since He stands on our side, who can do aught unto us? It is manifest that He is for us, and not against us.

32. He that spared not his own Son, but delivered him up for us all, how shall he not with him also freely give us all things?

>   *delivered him up.*—He was not dear to Him in our case.

---

27. [1] What the Spirit desireth.—Rh. V.

for us all.—Not for one or two did He suffer, but for all; [and] though Judas and the Jews were engaged in His betrayal, His coming would not have availed us had not the Heavenly Father delivered Him up.[1]

33. Who shall lay anything to the charge of God's elect? It is God that justifieth.[2]

lay anything.—Is it God? Is this likely of Him? Nay, it is not likely, for "He who justifieth" is more likely to pardon than to condemn.

34. Who is he that condemneth? It is Christ[3] that died, yea rather, that is risen again, who is even at the right hand of God, who also maketh intercession for us.

Christ.—Is it Jesus Christ? Will He at the same time redeem and accuse us? Not so. That will not be. That is not the love He has for us.

intercession.—He mediates; that is, the manhood which He received from us makes supplication to the Deity that we may not die.

35. Who shall separate us from the love of Christ? Shall tribulation, or distress, or persecution, or famine, or nakedness, or peril, or sword?

sword.—As he proved in his own person.[4]

36. As it is written, For thy sake we are killed all the day long; we are accounted as sheep for the slaughter.

killed.—As we are ready every day to undergo martyrdom.

like sheep.—It is lawful for everyone to slay us: we are not permitted to defend ourselves. (Pelagius.)

---

32. [1] See Acts ii. 23; John xix. 11.
33. [2] Shall God that justifieth?—R.V., margin.
34. [3] Shall Jesus Christ?—R. V., margin. The Latin has "simul autem" before "Jesus Christus," differing here from the Vulgate.
35. [4] St. Paul is said to have been beheaded, and is therefore represented in art as holding a sword. In an Irish poem in the Harleian MS., 1802, on the deaths of Christ and His Apostles, the following lines occur:—

"A sword-edge to slay Paul;
It was a tragical death, shameless, unjust."

38. For I am persuaded, that neither death, nor life, nor angels, nor principalities, nor powers, nor things present, nor things to come.

angels.—[If an angel were] present and made promises to us, and the [alternative] were that an angel should be guilty of falsehood, or that I should be separated from Christ, the former would be more likely than the latter.

CHAP. IX.

1. I say the truth in Christ, I lie not, my conscience also bearing me witness in the Holy Ghost.

I lie not.—It is a noble position in which I make this statement, [for it is] because I am a member of Christ.
bearing me witness.—My conscience does not deceive me, for it is the Holy Ghost in whom I bear witness.

2. That I have great heaviness and continual sorrow in my heart.

continual sorrow.—From of old and to this present time I have loved you.

3. For I could wish that myself were accursed from Christ for my brethren, my kinsmen according to the flesh.
accursed.—That is a captive.[1]

4. Who are Israelites; to whom pertaineth the adoption, and the glory, and the covenants, and the giving of the law, and the service of God, and the promises.

adoption.—Of the Israelites, whom God chose as His sons, according to the words, "Israel is my firstborn." (Exod. iv. 22.)

3.[1] The captive in heathen times was ἀνάθεμα, when slain as an offering to the gods. See on chap. xii. 3.

5. Whose are the fathers, and of whom as concerning the flesh Christ came, who is over all, God blessed for ever.[1]

Christ came.—It is hard to dishonour them, for Christ is one of them.
over all.—He is the chief of all.
God.—He is God, blessed for ever.

8. They which are the children of the flesh, these are not the children of God; but the children of the promise are counted for the seed.

flesh.—Like Ishmael and the unbelieving Israelites, they shall not receive the inheritance, because they are not the sons of promise.

11. For the children being not yet born, neither having done any good or evil, that the purpose of God according to election might stand, not of works, but of him that calleth.

purpose.—God's purpose was the election of one through mercy, [and] the condemnation of the other by a just judgment.

13. As it is written, Jacob have I loved, but Esau have I hated.

hated.—That is, by a judgment which was his due, for it was hatred both merited if mercy had not come, *i.e.*, it is not natural to him to feel hatred.

14. What shall we say then? Is there unrighteousness with God? God forbid.

unrighteousness.—Because He chose one of the two men without merit, and hated the other, does that seem unjust of God? No, it is not unrighteous.

---

5. [1] Here Pelagius enumerates several heretics against whom this verse was an argument: " Contra Manichæum, Photinum, et Arium ;" to which Primasius adds : " Contra Nestorium ;" but the Irish commentator omits all as unnecessary in Ireland.

16. So then it is not of him that willeth, nor of him that runneth, but of God that sheweth mercy.

   mercy.—He spares whomsoever is pleasing to Him.
   willeth.—The will is not profitable unless it proceeds from God; so also with " him that runneth," he does not profit unless God shews him mercy.

19. Thou wilt say unto me, Why doth he yet find fault? for who hath resisted his will?

   find fault.—This represents the opinions of those who used to say—" A man is not responsible for his sin : he does not deserve God's vengeance, for it is not easy to resist his will, for 'whom he will he hardeneth.' The matter, therefore, is not in our power."

20. Nay but, O man, who art thou that repliest against God? Shall the thing formed say to him that formed it, Why hast thou made me thus?

   Who art thou?—Why shouldst thou engage, in the interpretation of God's judgments, with Him?
   made me thus.—That is, Thou hast not made me well.

22. Endured with much long-suffering the vessels of wrath fitted for destruction.

   endured.—He did not take immediate vengeance on them, though they deserved it.
   fitted.—They were fit to take vengeance on them.

23. That he might make known the riches of his glory on the vessels of mercy, which he had afore prepared unto glory.

   vessels.—Not from goodness towards them (vessels of wrath) does He delay, but that He may bestow glory on His saints at such a time as He thinks advisable.
   of mercy.—Those for whom He destined mercy.
   unto glory.—Unto their salvation, though they deserved it not.

24. Even us, whom he hath called, not of the Jews only, but also of the Gentiles.

    called.—It is not the elect of the Jews only who shall enter into that glory; there shall also be faithful Gentiles. Your own brother, Hosea, O Jews, foretold the admission and election of the Gentiles. (Hosea ii. 23.)

26. In the place where it was said unto them, Ye are not my people, there shall they be called the children of the living God.

    place.—That is, the place of Scripture; or [the place in which] they shall be called; or [the place in which] they shall not be known by your name, *i.e.*, God's people.

27. Esaias also crieth concerning Israel, Though the number of the children of Israel be as the sand of the sea, a remnant shall be saved.

    crieth.—This is an address to the Gentiles. It was foretold to Israel that though they were multitudes, few of them would believe.

    remnant.—There will be some portion of them saved, but not all; for unto it (the remnant) will come the word[1] which perfects the man in righteousness and good works.

28. For he will finish the work,[1] and cut it short in righteousness: because a short work[2] will the Lord make upon the earth.

    in righteousness.—Those who believe will be righteous.

30. What shall we say then? That the Gentiles, which followed not after righteousness, have attained to righteousness, even the righteousness which is of faith.

    to righteousness.—The Gentiles obtained not their justification by merit. He points out afterwards two laws and two righteousnesses.

---

27. [1] See note to next verse.
28. [2] Will execute his word.—R.V. Shall finish his word.— Rh. V.

33. As it is written, Behold, I lay in Sion a stumblingstone and rock of offence : and whosoever believeth on him shall not be ashamed.

a stumblingstone.—This is a name for Christ.

rock of offence.—The nature of this stone is that many blows[1] are given to it; and he who falls on it breaks his bones, but he on whom it falls[2] perishes. Thus Christ is the corner-stone.

CHAP. X.

1. Brethren, my heart's desire and prayer to God for Israel is, that they might be saved.

desire.—He addresses this to the Gentiles, that they might not suppose He did not love the Jews, and desire their salvation.

4. For Christ is the end of the law for righteousness to every one that believeth.

for righteousness.—Every one who believes in Christ shall be righteous.

6. The righteousness which is of faith speaketh on this wise, Say not in thine heart, Who shall ascend into heaven ? (that is, to bring Christ down from above.)

righteousness.—He describes the righteousness which is of faith.

ascend.—To seek for other testaments (commandments[3]); this is the peculiar province of Paul.[4] Paul explains a text of the Old Testament.

to bring down Christ.—There is no need; He is come already.

7. Or, Who shall descend into the deep ? (that is, to bring up Christ again from the dead.)

to bring up Christ.—It is not necessary to bring Him up; He has already risen from the dead. It is sufficient for us, therefore, to believe in His Incarnation and Resurrection.

---

33. [1] See Isaiah l. 6; Matt. xxvi. 67.
33. [2] Matthew xxi. 44.
6. [3] Deut. xxx. 12, 13.   [4] 2 Cor. xii. 2.

8. But what saith it? The word is nigh thee, even in thy mouth, and in thy heart: that is, the word of faith, which we preach.

nigh thee.—Christ is at hand with His Gospel.

10. For with the heart man believeth unto righteousness; and with the mouth confession is made unto salvation.

believeth.—Belief in the heart makes the man righteous. Confession in the mouth makes the man safe (saved). Through these two means a man becomes righteous, and is saved,[1] so that he may be so for ever.

14. How shall they call on him in whom they have not believed? and how shall they believe in him of whom they have not heard? and how shall they hear without a preacher?

preacher.—He says this in the person of the Jew. It was wonderful to them that the Gentiles should be believers, for the prophets did not prophesy to them.

15. And how shall they preach except they be sent? as it is written, How beautiful are the feet of them that preach the gospel of peace, and bring glad tidings of good things!

sent.—They were not sent to them at all.

Gospel of peace.—It is deemed necessary that those who preach and negociate peace with kings should wear sandals of a peculiar kind, that it may be said "These men have come on an errand of peace." So must the acts of preachers have a special character.

good things.—That is, the Divine mysteries.

16. But they have not all obeyed the Gospel. For Esaias saith, Lord, who hath believed our report?[2]

not all.—Not many have believed what we heard from Thee, O God, or what all heard from us.

---

10. [1] "Safe and righteous" in the original; the order being inverted, as so often elsewhere in this Commentary.

16. [2] "Auditui nostro," which may mean, as in the gloss, "the thing heard, or our report." From the Septuagint of Isaiah liii. 1; it may mean either hearing or report. (Bishop Lightfoot.)

18. But I say, Have they not heard? Yes verily, their sound went into all the earth, and their words unto the ends of the world.

> *not heard.*—Is it not false of you, O Jews, to say that the Gentiles would not hear the prophecies regarding Christ? Nay, they have heard them.

19. But I say, Did not Israel know? First Moses saith, I will provoke you to jealousy by them that are no people, and by a foolish nation I will anger you.

> *know.*—That the Gentiles would be called to the faith. (Pelagius.) It is nobler for you what I say. Israel knew also that the Gentiles would be believers.
> *Moses.*—Your own leader says it at first.
> *to jealousy.*—That is, ye shall be jealous of the Gentiles being called to the faith; or, it refers to emulation: you shall emulate them in the reception of the faith.
> *no people.*—A people who were not hitherto mine until they became believers.

20. Esaias is very bold.

> *bold.*—He dares to say anything, because he is not afraid of the Jewish people.

21. But to Israel he saith, All day long I have stretched forth my hands unto a disobedient and gainsaying people.

> *all day long.*—To chide the Israelites he says this, lest they should boast of the prophets having been sent to them.

CHAP. XI.

1. I say then, Hath God cast away his people? God forbid. For I also am an Israelite, of the seed of Abraham, of the tribe of Benjamin.

> *cast away.*—[No] as is evident from this that He has not cast me away, and yet I truly am an Israelite.
> *Abraham.*—He is the foundation of my clan.

2. God hath not cast away his people which he foreknew. Wot ye not what the scripture saith of Elias? how he maketh intercession to God against Israel.
his people.—That is, those of them who should believe.
wot ye not.—Have ye not heard, O Gentiles, where it is written in the Books of Kings[1] concerning Elias.
maketh intercession to God.—To inflict vengeance on them.

3. I am left alone, and they seek my life.
my life.—That even this one person should not worship God.

4. But what saith the answer of God unto him? I have reserved to myself seven thousand men, who have not bowed the knee to Baal.
seven thousand.—Not thee alone, though thou sayest it.

6. And if by grace, then is it no more of works; otherwise grace is no more grace. But if it be of works, then is it no more grace; otherwise work is no more work.
by grace.—If it is grace, works have not preceded it.
no more grace.—It is debt, if works have preceded it.

7. What then? Israel hath not obtained that which he seeketh for; but the election hath obtained it, and the rest were blinded.
the election.—Those whom God elected by grace, not through the works of the Law, like the Gentiles.[2]
blinded.—That is the Jews. They attained not righteousness through grace.

8. (According as it is written, God hath given them the spirit of slumber, eyes that they should not see, and ears that they should not hear;) unto this day.
eyes.—The eyes of the inner man. That is, their reason was left under the guidance of their own will, and it was not good for them to be thus given up.[3]

9. And David saith, Let their table be made a snare, and a trap, and a stumbling-block, and a recompence unto them.
table.[4]—The altar on which they made offerings to their idols.

---

2. [1] 1 Kings xix. 10, 18.
7. [2] Chap. ii. 14, 15.   [3] Chap. i. 28.   [4] *Mensa.*

11. I say then, Have they stumbled that they should fall? God forbid; but rather through their fall salvation is come unto the Gentiles, for to provoke them to jealousy.

should fall.—So that they should never rise again? No, their fall is not so great as that.

stumbled.—He enquires have they stumbled so greatly as all to fall away from the faith of Christ. He replies, No; this is to encourage the Jews.

salvation.—God chose the Gentiles because the Jews did not value belief, but chose unbelief.

12. Now if the fall of them be the riches of the world, and the diminishing of them the riches of the Gentiles; how much more their fulness!

the world.—The people of the Gentiles.

their fulness.—If they were all[1] [believers], and not the Apostles only.

14. If by any means I may provoke to emulation them which are my flesh, and might save some of them.

save some.—Through my example; that is, that they may be moved to jealousy at my being in the faith, and perchance may imitate me.

15. For if the casting away of them be the reconciling of the world, what shall the receiving of them be but life from the dead?

life.—That the [Gentiles] should be alive in faith from the dead; that is, that they were dead in sin before.

16. For if the first-fruit be holy, the lump is also holy; and if the root be holy, so are the branches.

first-fruit.—That is Christ;[2] or the Apostle himself.

18. Boast not against the branches. But if thou boast, thou bearest not the root, but the root thee.

boast not.—Rejoice not, O Gentiles, that they were broken off and destroyed, for you are near them (in your state).

---

1. [1] Or if they were an entire nation restored to their full complement.
16. [2] Hic primitias Christum dicit, massam autem populum Hebræum a quibus Christus secundum carnem est. (Pelagius.)

20. Because of unbelief they were broken off, and thou standest by faith. Be not high-minded, but fear.

by faith.—Because it was freely, and not by merit, thou wast grafted in. I have a friend's advice for thee, O Gentile, that thou shouldst not be proud, and shouldst be constant in the faith.

fear.—Lest thou be cast away from the truth through pride, like the original clan (the Jews).

24. If thou wert cut out of the olive tree, which is wild by nature, and wert graffed contrary to nature into a good olive tree.

graffed.—He uses a simile here; for they have a custom of making an incision in a tree, and inserting [a cutting of] another tree in it.

25. Blindness in part is happened to Israel, until the fulness of the Gentiles be come in.

blindness in part.—It was a part of them [only] that believed not, and even they will soon become believers; or, "blindness" here means stupidity. "In part," that is, from a little while: *Ex parte contigit*, refers to time only, as Pelagius says.[1]

come in.—Till all the Gentiles are saved; or a portion of every nation.

28. As concerning the Gospel, they are enemies for your sakes: but as touching the election, they are beloved for the fathers' sakes.

your sakes.—That is the Gentiles. They love me not because I preach the Gospel to the Gentiles.

beloved.—They are indeed my friends; I love them; they are a clan chosen unto God.

29. The gifts and calling of God are without repentance.

gifts.—Remission of sins.

without repentance.—That is, what He promised He will not repent of.

---

25. [1] In tantum Israel et delicta et perfidia occuparunt *ut veniret tempus* quo gentes omnes admitterentur ad vitam et ita omnis Israel per fidem solam salvaretur. (Pelagius.)

31. Even so have these also now not believed, that through your mercy they also may obtain mercy.

>   *obtain mercy.*—It is by mercy they will be saved when they believe, not by merit, nor by the work of the law.

32. For God hath concluded[1] them all in unbelief, that he might have mercy upon all.

>   *concluded.*—Shut them up; that is, He found them all in unbelief. It was not by a compulsory shutting up, says Pelagius, but by a conclusion of reason.[2] To boast of one's merits is of no avail here, so that it was by God's mercy [alone] that they were saved.

33. O the depth of the riches both of the wisdom and knowledge of God! how unsearchable are his judgments, and his ways past finding out!

>   *ways past finding out.*—Question: What are the Riches here, and the Wisdom, and the Knowledge, and the Unsearchable Judgments, and the Ways past finding out, and what the Mind of the Lord? It is not difficult to answer [say some]. All these things belong to the unspeakable secret meaning[3] which was in the mysteries of the Godhead in creating the elements, "in the beginning." (Genesis i. 1.) But it seems difficult [to suppose] a sudden transition[4] from ethics and the teaching of mankind to a statement about the creation of the elements. It is plain that he is following up his previous observations, and that what he admires here is the depth of the Divine knowledge shown in the salvation of mankind by mercy.

---

32. [1] Shut up.—R. V.
32. [2] The words are the beginning of a note of Pelagius, which is as follows:—' Non vi conclusit sed ratione conclusit quos invenit in incredulitate: hoc est Judæos omnes et gentes hic conclusit." Primasius, in copying the note, omits the words quoted in the gloss, which savoured of Pelagius's peculiar opinions.
33. [3] See Appendix.
33. [4] Literally, It does not seem easy to leap.

CHAP. XII.

1. I beseech you, therefore, brethren, by the mercies of God, that ye present your bodies a living sacrifice, holy, acceptable unto God, which is your reasonable service.[1]

    acceptable to God.—Pure and free from sin; that is, from all vices, for the soul is ready to do the will of God; let the soul, therefore, be stirred up to do good.
    holy.—As the [victim] offered under the law before the door of the temple was without any appearance of blemish, [so be ye] without any appearance of sin.
    service (or, *worship*).—Let every prayer you offer according to God's will be a lawful prayer.

2. Be ye transformed by the renewing of your mind, that ye may prove what is that good, and acceptable, and perfect will of God.

    renewing.—Let your minds be wise, not as they were before.
    will of God.—The will of God, then, has three characteristics; it is good, and acceptable, and perfect; and these are the same as the three things mentioned before, a sacrifice living, holy, acceptable.

3. For I say, through the grace given unto me, to every man that is among you, not to think of himself more highly[2] than he ought to think; but to think soberly,[3] according as God hath dealt to every man the measure of faith.

    think more highly (or, *to be more wise*).—He means by being "more wise," doing what He forbids, and by being "wise unto sobriety," abstaining from doing what He forbids, and fulfilling His commandments.
    the measure.—As He bestows it (wisdom) on every man, according to his faith.

---

1. [1] Worship.—R.V., margin.
3. [2] *Plus sapere*—to be more wise.— Rh. V.
3. [3] *Sapere ad prudentiam*—to be wise unto sobriety.- Rh. V.

4. For as we have many members in one body, and all members have not the same office.

same office.—We cannot see except with our eyes, and so on: all the members perform a single work or a single service.

5. So we, being many, are one body in Christ, and every one members one of another.

body.—We are a body to Christ, and He is a head to us.

6. Having then gifts differing according to the grace that is given to us, whether prophecy, let us prophesy according to the proportion of faith.

gifts.—That which causes the co-operation is that every one's gift is different.

given to us.—As every one had a portion of Divine grace.

prophecy.—Let it be according to the rule of faith, not like the false prophets, whose prophesying transgressed the faith.

7. Or ministry, let us wait on our ministering; or he that teacheth, on teaching.

ministering.—That is, in obedience to every one.

teacheth.—"Let every man abide in the same calling wherein he was called." (1 Cor. vii. 20.) Or [it means] preaching to every one after baptism; let [this] be instructive; that is, let the teacher act up to it, and show an example to every one.

8. He that exhorteth, on exhortation; he that giveth, let him do it with simplicity; he that ruleth, with diligence; he that sheweth mercy, with cheerfulness.

exhorteth.—Strengthening every one.

cheerfulness.—For "God loveth a cheerful giver." (2 Cor. ix. 7.)

11. Fervent in spirit.

fervent.—So that courage from the love of the Spirit be in us.

12. Rejoicing in hope; patient in tribulation; continuing instant in prayer.

hope.—The glory to come strengthens our hope.
prayer.—Let us be constant in prayer, that we may be able to bear trials.

14. Bless them which persecute you: bless, and curse not.

bless.—It is not sufficient to bless if you [also] curse, nor is it sufficient to abstain from cursing unless you also bless.

16. Be of the same mind one toward another. Mind not high things, but condescend to men of low estate.[1] Be not wise in your own conceits.

same mind.—Let the joy or the sorrow be as though it happened to yourselves.
low estate (or, *things*).—Occupy yourselves with every humble work.

17. Recompense to no man evil for evil. Provide things honest in the sight of all men.

recompense to no man.—For that is the true wisdom.
all men.—" That they may see your good works" (Matt. v. 16); that is, the doing of good actions to them.

18. If it be possible, as much as lieth in you, live peaceably with all men.

live peaceably.—In whatever way, have peace with every one, even your persecutors.

19. Dearly beloved, avenge[2] not yourselves.

avenge not.—Let it not be your own strength that defends you, lest anger take possession of you: or [remember] " Whosoever shall smite thee on thy right cheek, turn to him the other also." (Matt. v. 39.)

---

16. [1] Things that are lowly.—R.V.
19. [2] *defendentes.*

21. Be not overcome of evil, but overcome evil with good.

> *overcome evil.*—Do not enter into a contest with him in evil, lest you both be evil together. According to Pelagius, he is said to have overcome who has brought the other over to his own side. Thou shouldst do good to him, and then he will be good.

CHAP. XIII.

1. Let every soul be subject to the higher powers. For there is no power but of God: the powers that be are ordained of God.

> *no power.*—For he does not consider a wicked power to be a power at all.
>
> *ordained.*—It is God that ordained the powers; or, the powers that are of God are [duly] ordained.

3. For rulers are not a terror to good works, but to the evil. Wilt thou then not be afraid of the power? do that which is good, and thou shalt have praise of the same.

> *terror.*—It is more reasonable that he should be a terror to evil deeds; for the office of a ruler is to increase good deeds, and to abate evil deeds. He declares here the powers to which service should be rendered, viz., those that correct the evil and magnify the good.
>
> *praise of the same.*—Thou shalt have from him the reward of thy good deeds. Origen says: "Thou shalt receive praise from God if thou art subject unto kings for His sake."

8. Owe no man anything, but to love one another: for he that loveth another hath fulfilled the law.

> *owe no man.*—For nothing is owed to you: put away all debts, that you may be free to exercise charity.

11. And that, knowing the time, that now it is high time to awake out of sleep; for now is our salvation nearer than when we believed.

> *the time.*—It is the time for doing good; or [it means] the time of the New Testament; or [the time] when the love of our neighbour is the fulfilling of the law.

12. The night is far spent, the day is at hand : let us therefore cast off the works of darkness, and let us put on the armour of light.

armour.—Whether we are called to active warfare or passive endurance.

13. Let us walk honestly as in the day; not in rioting and drunkenness, not in chambering and wantonness, not in strife and envying.

walk.—Let our walk be honest, as in the day ; for it is by day we travel and see our path.

14. Put ye[1] on the Lord Jesus Christ, and make not provision for the flesh, to fulfil the lusts thereof.

put ye on.—Be ye raiment for the Lord, that He may dwell in you ; or, let Christ be raiment for you.

CHAP. XIV.

1. Him that is weak in the faith receive ye, but not to doubtful disputations.

receive ye.—Not to pass judgment on him.

disputations.—Let it not be your opinion that his state [of mind] is not good.

2. For one believeth that he may eat all things ; another, who is weak, eateth herbs.

all things.—His faith is strong ; he regards every food as pure. (1 Tim. iv. 4.)

herbs.—He eats bread only, and he prefers it, like Daniel and the three children. (Daniel i. 12.)

3. God hath received him.

received him.—He has called him as well as thee. He values him as much as thee.

---

14. [1] *Induite vos Dominum :* this admits of either of the above translations.

5. One man esteemeth one day above another: another esteemeth every day alike. Let every man be fully persuaded in his own mind.

every day.—These make no difference between days, but practise abstinence always.

persuaded.—Let each do what seems good to him if he does it for God's sake.

6. He that eateth not, to the Lord he eateth not, and giveth God thanks.

eateth not.—He who fasts.

8. Whether we live therefore, or die, we are the Lord's.

the Lord's.—None of us belongs to another. We all belong to God. We must not find fault with Him, though our life and death are in His hands; for to this end Christ both died, and rose, and revived, that He might be Lord both of the dead and the living. (See verse 9.)

10. But why dost thou judge thy brother? or why dost thou set at nought thy brother? for we shall all stand before the judgment seat of Christ.[1]

judge.—He may be a good man, though he eats not of every kind of food: he may be a good man, though he does eat his food.

Christ (or, *God*).—For there is a Judge apart from you, that is, God. He is wise in the matter, not like you.

15. Destroy not him with thy meat for whom Christ died.

destroy not.—Put away from thee luxurious diet, and live on the same food as thy nation, so that thou mayest not need indulgence from him.

Christ died.—Christ has suffered more for him, even death; therefore put from thee the food in which thou delightest.

---

10. [1] God.—R.V.

17. For the kingdom of God is not meat and drink; but righteousness, and peace, and joy in the Holy Ghost.

> *meat and drink.*—It is not this that will bring you to heaven, though it may be proper food.

19. Let us therefore follow after the things which make for peace, and things wherewith one may edify another.

> *peace.*—This he says to shield those who abstain from certain kinds of food.

21. It is good neither to eat flesh, nor to drink wine, nor any thing whereby thy brother stumbleth, or is offended, or is made weak.

> *weak.*—His abstinence is weakened.

22. Hast thou faith? have it to thyself before God. Happy is he that condemneth not himself in that thing which he alloweth.

> *faith.*—We know it is the perfection of thy faith which impels thee to what thou doest.

CHAP. XV.

2. Let every one of us please his neighbour for his good to edification.

> *his good.*—Charity, or the love of our neighbour, edifies. (1 Cor. viii. 1.)

3. For even Christ pleased not himself; but, as it is written, The reproaches of them that reproached thee fell on me.

> *pleased not.*—It was not for His own pleasure He suffered, but for our advantage, Pelagius says. It is not more trying for you than for Christ;[1] for He underwent great sufferings, in obedience to His Father.

---

[1] The allusion appears to be to St. Matthew x. 24—"The disciple is not above his master, nor the servant above his lord." This passage from Pelagius is not in Migne, but the following expresses the thought: "Imitatur hoc et discipulus Christi, non quærit suum commodum. Ille enim ob aliorum salutem etiam mortuus est." For some further remarks, see Appendix.

4. Whatsoever things were written aforetime were written for our learning.

written.—For they needed not to write them, unless it were to give us strength in times of trial.

5. Now the God of patience and consolation grant you to be likeminded one toward another, according to Christ Jesus.

likeminded.—That every one may love the other according to the command of Jesus :[1] or, according to the example of Jesus Christ.

6. That ye may with one mind and one mouth glorify God, even the Father of our Lord Jesus Christ.

one mind.—That you may have one mind as to Him, and one act, even an act of love.

8. Now I say that Jesus Christ was a minister of the circumcision for the truth of God.

minister.—It was through humility He took that office on Him.

truth of God.—To show forth that He is true God, and that it is He who was foretold by the Patriarchs, [saying] that the Son would be like the Father, and that His appearance should be that of His nation. (Deut. xviii. 15.)

9. And that the Gentiles might glorify God for his mercy, as it is written.

glorify.—They worship God; in return He bestows on them the good gift of mercy.

written.—It was foretold long ago that the Gentiles would be worshippers of God.

12. Esaias saith, There shall be a root of Jesse, and he that shall rise to reign over the Gentiles; in him shall the Gentiles trust.

a root.—That is Christ, who is Himself the root of Jesse, according to the Divine nature; for He Himself formed Jesse, and from Jesse again He derived His origin according to the flesh.

---

5. [1] John xiii. 35.

13. Now the God of hope fill you with all joy and peace in believing, that ye may abound in hope, through the power of the Holy Ghost.
 hope.—It is He that strengthens us, that we may abide in perfect hope.

15. Because of the grace that is given to you of God.
 grace.—The grace of teaching; or [the grace] of preaching, for it was to preach to all that I received this grace.

19. So that from Jerusalem, and round about unto Illyricum, I have fully preached the gospel of Christ.
 Illyricum.—A region between Italy and Greece: west of Greece and east of Italy.

21. As it is written, To whom he was not spoken of, they shall see.
 written.—It is of me it was foretold that the Gentiles should see by me (though no tidings had come to them) the things concerning Him.

30. That ye strive together with me in your prayers to God for me.
 strive.—Here it is shown that mutual intercession is right.

CHAP. XVI.

2. That ye receive her in the Lord, as becometh saints.
 becometh saints.—In the way that is proper and fit for saints; that is, in the Lord—as saints should receive saints.

3. Greet[1] Priscilla and Aquila, my helpers in Christ Jesus.
 greet (or, *salute*).—It is always a sign of good-will and peace when the word "salute" occurs; that is, let there be peace to you from them, and do you salute them.

4. Who have for my life laid down their own necks: unto whom not only I give thanks, but also all the churches of the Gentiles.
 laid down.—That is, in persecutions; they were ready to undergo martyrdom for my sake.
 churches.—Those to whom I preached the faith.

---

3. [1] Salute.—R.V. and Rhemish.

5. Likewise greet the church that is in their house. Salute my well-beloved Epænetus, who is the first-fruits of Achaia unto Christ.

>   *church in their house.*—That is, the family of Priscilla and Aquila.
>   *first-fruits.*—He is the first-fruits of belief in Asia; or, in Asia itself he gave his first-fruits in believing to Christ; or, "from the first," that is, he was the first man of the people of Asia who believed in Christ; or, it refers to rank, that is, he was one of the chiefs of Asia[1] who believed in Christ.

6. Greet Mary, who bestowed much labour on us.
>   *labour.*—Confirming everything that was preached to you.

7. Salute Andronicus and Junia, my kinsmen, and my fellow-prisoners, who are of note[2] among the apostles.
>   *of note* (or, *noble*).—That is, by birth; or, their apostleship was noble because they received Christ, and were of His household, not like me; or, they were helpers of the apostles.

17. Now I beseech you, brethren, mark them which cause offences.
>   *offences* (or, *divisions*).—That is not what you read of in the Gospel.

18. By good words and fair speeches deceive the hearts of the simple.
>   *fair speeches.*—That is, says Pelagius, by blandishments and flatteries, with feigned discourse; the preaching is delightful and beautiful, but its meaning is poisonous.

---

5 [1] The Asiarchs, or chief officers of Asia, who were magistrates in the Eastern part of the Roman Empire.
7. [2] *Nobiles.*

19. For your obedience is come abroad unto all men. I am glad therefore on your behalf.

> *obedience.*—Evident is your submission to good and evil; therefore they endeavour to subject you to their doctrine; or, evident is your obedience to the faith and the Gospel: therefore [he says] "I beseech you," &c. (*v.* 17.)
>
> *glad.*—For evident is your fame; or, he says this lest he should offend them, because he said they were obedient, that is, easily yielding to seductive influences.

21. Timotheus my workfellow.

> *workfellow.*—That is, in the preaching of the Gospel.

23. Gaius mine host,[1] and of the whole church, saluteth you. Erastus the chamberlain[2] of the city saluteth you.

> *host* (or, *guest*).—Who lately came to me[3] [as guest]; or, Paul was a guest of his.
>
> *the whole church.*—The whole congregation of the saints on earth: that is, all the people mentioned and the united church are two things, and he himself is the third.[4]
>
> *chamberlain* (or, *treasurer*).—The man in charge of the treasure-house; or, the guardian; or, one who was formerly the steward of the city, but now he guards the faith.

25. The revelation of the mystery, which was kept secret since the world began.

> *mystery.*—That is, of your salvation; or, of the incarnation of Christ; or, that some proselytes, that is, foreigners, are to be admitted to the faith.

---

23. [1] *Hospes.*   [2] *Treasurer.*—R.V. and Rhemish.
[3] Acts xx. 4.
23. [4] That is, there is a threefold salutation, the name Tertius (*v.* 22) being translated as if it meant "Third." The writer of this gloss was misled by the Latin translation, which reads, "And the whole Church," instead of "And *of* the whole Church."

27. To God only wise, be glory through Jesus Christ for ever.

only wise.—He knows the obedience and faith of each; or, to Him should glory be given, because from Him proceeds all wisdom.

Jesus Christ.—Through the incarnation of Jesus Christ the Gentiles have become obedient to the faith.

---

1 CORINTHIANS.

CHAP. I.

3. Grace be unto you, and peace, from God our Father, and from the Lord Jesus Christ.

grace.—We pray for this; he says "we," for the Epistle was sent by two persons, Paul and Sosthenes.

4. I thank my God always on your behalf, for the grace of God which is given you by Jesus Christ.

I thank my God.—It is a marvel to me that you have God's grace.

7. So that ye come behind in no gift; waiting for the coming[1] of our Lord Jesus Christ.

coming (or, *revelation*).—You know the first Advent by the Gospel; you will know the second Advent by revelation.[2]

9. God is faithful, by whom ye were called unto[3] the fellowship of his Son Jesus Christ our Lord.

fellowship.—In the unity of the Body of Christ; that you also may be sons of God.

---

7. [1] Revelation.—R.V. See 2 Thess. i. 7, R.V.
7. [2] Revelatio autem dicitur Domini adventus, quia modo a nobis abscondita est. (Pelagius.)
9. [3] Into.—R.V.

10. I beseech you, brethren, by the name of our Lord Jesus Christ, that ye all speak the same thing.

> *brethren.*—He addresses them as brethren, that they might not say it was from hatred he blamed them, but from love.
>
> *same thing.*—That they should have one faith. Here he comes to the bitter draught of blame, when the mouth of the cup had been previously anointed with honey, that is with the gentle and friendly words he spoke to them. Here then is shown the cause why this Epistle was written. There were great contentions and discord among the disciples, but there was unity among the teachers. All, indeed, were the servants of God, but the disciples made distinctions between them, and treated them as gods; this is what he blames here.

11. For it hath been declared unto me of you, my brethren, by them which are of the house of Chloe, that there are contentions among you.

> *contentions.*—They are not secular quarrels [which are meant].

13. Is Christ divided? was Paul crucified for you? or were ye baptized in the name of Paul?

> *divided.*—Yes, says Pelagius, the body is divided when the members disagree; that is, when the respect due to the head is given to the members.
>
> *was Paul crucified?*—I will begin with myself.
>
> *baptized.*—Why then, was the worship due to God given to Paul in that way?

14. I thank God that I baptized none of you, but Crispus and Gaius.

> *Crispus.*—And they do not say that they were baptized in my name.

17. For Christ sent me not to baptize, but to preach the gospel: not with wisdom of words, lest the cross of Christ should be made of none effect.

> *preach.*—As He said, "To bear my name before the Gentiles." (Acts ix. 15.) Preaching, therefore, was his duty,

and the awakening [of the people], so that every one should be ready for his baptism, and his (Paul's) disciple for [the performance of] it after; so that he should not be injured by what others have done.

cross of Christ.—In which you glory. It is not that I would not do it, but the mystery of the cross would not be understood if the preaching were eloquent and brilliant. Cross is the name of the act of crucifixion, and it is transferred from it to the tree itself.

21. For after that in the wisdom of God the world by wisdom knew not God, it pleased God by the foolishness of preaching to save them that believe.

knew not God.—Recognised Him not in the elements (*i.e.*, in creation); or, in all wisdom. There is a divine wisdom they cannot understand by their own [natural] wisdom.

22. The Jews require a sign, and the Greeks seek after wisdom.

sign.—They do not value preaching unless miracles accompany it.

wisdom.—They do not value wisdom unless eloquence accompanies it.

25. Because the foolishness of God is wiser than men; and the weakness of God is stronger than men.

wiser.—What men could not attain through their own wisdom till He came [they can now] through His cross. That is, what Jews and Greeks sought after, viz., virtue and wisdom, they would find, if they believed, as they understand who are called.[1]

26. For you see your calling, brethren, how that not many wise men after the flesh, not many mighty, not many noble, are called.

brethren.—O all ye faithful!

wise after the flesh.—They would not be really wise if they were after the flesh.

---

25. [1] 2 Peter i. 3.

called.—They are not all wise; that is, not many of them are; or, not many of them are powerful, if it is according to the flesh; for he [only] is wise, and powerful, and mighty, and noble, who believes in Jesus Christ, and what He teaches.

CHAP. II.

3. I was with you in weakness, and in fear, and in much trembling.

weakness.—Weakness and great fear become a servant (slave) while he is in the service of his master.

5. That your faith should not stand in the wisdom of men, but in the power of God.

faith.—Let not your trust be in philosophy.

6. Howbeit we speak wisdom among them that are perfect; yet not the wisdom of this world,[1] nor of the princes of this world,[1] that come to nought.

to nought.—They are coming to nought with their wisdom through our Gospel, as Pelagius says; or, their bodies and souls will be separated; or, their wisdom will depart from them.

7. We speak the wisdom of God in a mystery, even the hidden wisdom.

hidden.—From the unbelievers, says Pelagius, so that none of the wise ones of the world knows it.

11. For what man knoweth the things of a man, save the spirit of man which is in him? even so the things of God knoweth no man, but the Spirit of God.

what man.—Here we have a similitude.

save the spirit of man.—Save his intellect; that is, the man himself.

in him.—In the man: he reflects on it (is conscious of it); so he in whom the Spirit of God is knows the mysteries of God.

---

[1] Age.—R.V., margin.

13. Which things also we speak, not in the words which man's wisdom teacheth, but which the Holy Ghost teacheth; comparing spiritual things with spiritual.

spiritual things (or, *men*).—That is, giving to each the teaching suitable to him.

14. But the natural man receiveth not the things of the Spirit of God; for they are foolishness unto him: neither can he know them, for they are spiritually discerned.[2]

natural man.—Who is like a quadruped.
foolishness.—Spiritual proof is not suited to him.
spiritually discerned (or, *judged*).—He is judged as regards the spirit, by God: or, by the spiritual man.

CHAP. III.

4. For while one saith, I am of Paul; and another, I am of Apollos; are ye not carnal?

Apollos.—What kind of men are those you make gods[3] of? They are servants and ministers of Him in whom you believe.

10. According to the grace of God which is given unto me, as a wise master-builder, I have laid the foundation, and another buildeth thereon. But let every man take heed how he buildeth thereupon.

grace given.—Not according to my virtue, says Pelagius.
buildeth.—He to whom it has been preached builds thereon. My office is not to build on, but to lay the foundation.
take heed.—A building should be suitable to the foundation.[4]

11. For other foundation can no man lay than that is laid, which is Jesus Christ.

which is laid.—Though false apostles make it void.

---

13. [1] Interpreting spiritual things to spiritual men.—R.V., margin.
14. [2] Judged.—R.V.
4. [3] For a parallel, see Appendix.
10. [4] Id est ut superedificia congruant fundamento ne si obliqua fuerint et frivola ruinam faciant manente incolumi fundamento. (Hilary.)

14. If any man's work abide which he hath built thereupon, he shall receive a reward.

abide.—If he is constant in trials, and his acts are good.

15. If any man's work shall be burned, he shall suffer loss: but he himself shall be saved; yet so as by fire.

loss.—That is, of his reward, as he has not well guarded the flock.

saved.—He alone shall escape separated from his flock.

21. All things are yours.

yours.—We are your ministers, says Pelagius; you are the people of Christ alone: by "all things" he means the following.

22. Whether Paul, or Apollos, or Cephas, or the world, or life, or death, or things present, or things to come; all are yours.

things present.—This means life.
things to come.—This means death.

CHAP. IV.

3. With me it is a very small thing that I should be judged of you or of man's judgment:[1] yea, I judge not mine own self.

judgment (or, *day*).—Human praise is compared to a day on account of its shortness, as the Prophet says: "I have not desired the day of men" (that is, the praise). (Jeremiah xvii. 16, Vulgate.)

6. And these things, brethren, I have in a figure transferred to myself and to Apollos for your sakes; that ye might learn in us not to think of men above that which is written, that no one of you be puffed up for one against another.

---

3. [1] Day.—R.V., margin, and Rh. V.

your sakes.—Practise what I preach. I pronounce no judgment on any one, not [even] on myself; as though he said, for this reason I have in a figure transferred to myself all the things we have just spoken of. We have put ourselves in your power, and have said, We are your servants, and we do not glory in teachers like Gamaliel and others, nor have we judged any one until the Lord shall judge him. So that you may learn humility from me, so as not to boast of teachers, or to judge any one, whether he is good or bad, until God shall have judged him.

12. And labour, working with our own hands: being reviled, we bless; being persecuted, we suffer it.

labour.—Preaching was his work by day, and labouring with his hands by night.

13. Being defamed, we intreat: we are made as the filth of the world, and are the offscouring of all things unto this day.

offscouring.—That is, destruction. *Peripsema*, Pelagius says, is Greek, and means the very worst persons, or persons who are despised.

15. Though ye have ten thousand instructors[1] in Christ, yet have ye not many fathers: for in Christ Jesus I have begotten you through the gospel.

instructors.—Pedagogues, or guardians of boys; that is, the perfect folk[2] who attend at baptism.

CHAP. V.

3. For I verily, as absent in the body, but present in the spirit, have judged already, as though I were present, concerning him that hath so done this deed.

present.—He is present when his words are read.

---

15. [1] Tutors.—R.V. *Pedagogorum.*
15. [2] The perfect folk appear to be the same as the *Teleioi* mentioned by Bingham (Eccles. Antiq., Vol. I., 34, 39), who acted as sponsors. Amongst the ancients the "pedagogue" was entrusted with the moral supervision of the child. See also *teleiosis* in Littledale's Offices of Holy Eastern Church (Glossary).

4. In the name of our Lord Jesus Christ, when ye are gathered together, and my spirit, with the power of our Lord Jesus Christ.

>   *my spirit.*—[As shewn] in the judgment of those letters; or, it is by the [Holy] Spirit I have given my decision.

5. To deliver such an one unto Satan for the destruction of the flesh, that the spirit may be saved in the day of the Lord Jesus.

>   *such an one.*—I have judged to deliver him. [*i.e.*, either] I should have delivered him, or ye would have delivered him. Another interpretation is, that he is given up to madness,[1] so that thereby his soul may be saved in the day of the Lord.
>
>   *unto Satan.*—That is, to the adversary, *i.e.*, for repentance; he is so termed, because vice in his person is opposed to virtue.

7. Purge out therefore the leaven, that ye may be a new lump, as ye are unleavened. For even Christ our passover is sacrificed for us.

>   *leaven.*—As it was forbidden to put leaven in bread at the feast of the lamb (passover), so it is not right that there should be any of the leaven of sin in the feast of the Lamb,[2] *i.e.*, Christ.

---

5. [1] There were two interpretations of the words "delivering to Satan"—one which regarded them as another expression for excommunication. From this relief could be obtained by public penance.

The other, that of Augustine, Jerome, and others, was that in the Apostle's days there was, besides the spiritual censures, also a corporal power and possession (by Satan). (Bingham, v. 485.)

On the possible connexion between certain cases of insanity and demoniac possession, see Trench on the Miracles, 9th edition. "It may well be a question" (he says) "if an apostle were to enter into a madhouse now, he might not recognise some of the sufferers there as possessed."—p. 174.

7. [2] This expression recalls the usage of the Greek Church. Thus in the Liturgy of St. James the rubric is:—"And when he [the priest] signs the bread, he saith: Behold the Lamb of God, the Son of the Father, sacrificed for the life and salvation of the world."—Rev. J. M. Neale's *Primitive Liturgies*, p. 60. So in the Liturgy of St. Chrysostom, the Deacon says: "Sir, break the holy bread." And the priest, dividing it into four parts with care and reverence, saith: "The Lamb of God is broken and distributed."—p. 121.

8. Therefore let us keep the feast, not with the old leaven, neither with the leaven of malice and wickedness; but with the unleavened bread of sincerity and truth.

feast.—The feast of Christ.
truth.—Ours should be simplicity and truth, like Adam's, before he sinned.

10. Yet not altogether with the fornicators of this world, or with the covetous, or extortioners, or with idolaters; for then must ye needs go out of the world.

out of the world.—This appears to me a very plain declaration; for I know you will not be in communion with them further than you ought, for their ways are not yours. It is right, therefore, not to be intimate with them. But it would be better for us, says Pelagius, to depart from this life than to stand in need of a warning to separate us from association with the Gentiles. I did not mean this when I wrote to you not to keep company (*v.* 9). I do not desire you to separate from the Gentiles [altogether], because it affords an opportunity to preach to them if perchance they may be led to embrace the faith in anywise. Were it not for this, you ought to depart from the land and earth of those people; but the office[1] of preaching has constrained you, and you have gone [to them].

CHAP. VI.

2. Do ye not know that the saints shall judge the world? and if the world shall be judged by you, are ye unworthy to judge the smallest matters?

judge the world.—If you knew that, you would not deprive them of the judgment of small matters.
be judged.—By you [as judges]: or, by your example, as Pelagius says; that is, the judgment of this world will be in your power.

---

10. [1] Literally, the order of preaching.

3. Know ye not that we shall judge angels? how much more things that pertain to this life?

judge angels.—To the faithful [this is addressed]. The angels meant here are devils. For there was more reason that we should sin from the frail nature of the flesh which we received—if we should sin—than there was for them to have done so, from the finer nature they received.[1] For this reason it is that we shall be their judges. Or [it means], we shall judge the true angels, and this is the way in which we shall judge them: as they will be in the encompassment of the judgment, so shall we, as the Psalmist says: "He shall call heaven from above, and the earth to judge his people" (Psalm xlix. 4, Vulgate): or, it is spoken of Christ, who, in our human nature, shall judge the angels: or, the more exalted saints shall judge the lower.

11. And such were some of you: but ye are washed, but ye are sanctified, but ye are justified in the name of the Lord Jesus, and by the Spirit of our God.

such.—Such were your names: or, such were your works.

justified.—These three things belong to you, purity, and holiness, and righteousness, in the name of the Lord Jesus Christ, and of the Holy Ghost. Here he indicates the three Persons of the Trinity, the Father, the Son, and the Holy Ghost.

12. All things are lawful unto me, but all things are not expedient: all things are lawful for me, but I will not be brought under the power of any.

power.—I am not brought under the power of any of them for their satisfaction, as drunkards are placed under restraint from wine and other [stimulants].

---

3. [1] Angelos apostatas qui digni creati lapsi sunt, cum isti fragiles stent. (Glossa Ordinaria.)

Si angelos qui propriæ mentis pravitate ab ordine suo excederunt nos judicabimus aut arguemus qui corpora habemus: quia illi corporibus carentes suam non servaverunt legem, nos autem secundum datas nobis a domino leges conversati sumus. Si ergo inexcusabile constituemus peccatum illorum quanto magis idonei sumus qui humanas contentiones dissolvamus mutuasque inter nos causas ac lites. (Photius ap. Œcumenius in the Glossa Ordinaria.)

14. And God hath both raised up the Lord, and will also raise up us by his own power.

> *raise us up.*—Because we are members of Him. The body of which the Lord is head shall be raised up by the power of the Godhead as our Lord Jesus Christ was raised.

20. For ye are bought with a price: therefore glorify[1] God in your body and in your spirit, which are God's.

> *glorify [and bear] God.*—Let Him be the burthen you carry.

CHAP. VII.

7. For I would that all men were even as I myself. But every man hath his proper gift of God, one after this manner, and another after that.

> *as I.*—Although I wish it, perhaps all will not be like [me]. Yet though they do not resemble me in celibacy, let them all do so in [performing] the will of God, whether single or married.

9. It is better to marry than to burn.

> *better.*—Jerome says the former evil is to be preferred to the latter.

15. For the unbelieving husband is sanctified by the wife, and the unbelieving wife is sanctified by the husband: else were your children unclean, but now are they holy.

> *unclean.*—Unless this is done (*v.* 13), your children will be unclean; that is, those who cleave to the unbelieving [parent] will be unbelievers. Since, however, you keep together, and are now believers, your children also will be believers.

17. But as God hath distributed to every man, as the Lord hath called every one, so let him walk.

> *distributed.*—Whether it was in celibacy or marriage he was called, let him so remain.

---

20. [1] Glorify and bear God in your body.—Rh. V.

18. Is any man called being circumcised? let him not become uncircumcised. Is any called in uncircumcision? let him not be circumcised.

> *circumcised.*—In the condition of celibacy; that is, circumcised from marriage, for it is not of fleshly circumcision he is treating here, according to the [saying], "Virginity circumcises vices."
>
> *become uncircumcised.*—Let him not enter into matrimony. It is evident here that in what he said above he is not speaking of carnal circumcision; or, if his mind is circumcised, let it not seek uncircumcision.
>
> *let him not be circumcised.*—Let him not put away his wife: or, let him not say in his mind it would be better to do so.

21. Art thou called being a servant? care not for it: but if thou mayest be made free, use it rather.

> *care not for it.*—Do not seek for celibacy.
>
> *made free.*—Though thou couldst put away thy wife, thou shouldst not do so, but wait if perchance you could agree [to part].

22. For he that is called in the Lord, being a servant, is the Lord's freeman: likewise also he that is called, being free, is Christ's servant.

> *being a servant.*—It is in the marriage state he was called unto God.[1]
>
> *freeman.*—A free slave; that is, he is a freed man unto God; but he does not serve Him alone.
>
> *Christ's servant.*—He serves Christ alone, without a divided service to his wife.

25. Now concerning virgins I have no commandment of the Lord: yet I give my judgment, as one that hath obtained mercy of the Lord to be faithful.

> *my judgment.*—He did not say, let every one abide in celibacy, whether he is able or not. Question: What did the Lord say? The answer is not difficult. He said: "He that is able to receive it, let him receive it." (Matt. xix. 12.)

---

22. [1] Aliqui servitutem conjugium volunt intelligi. (Primasius.)

28. But and if thou marry, thou hast not sinned; and if a virgin marry, she hath not sinned. Nevertheless such shall have trouble in the flesh: but I spare you.

trouble.—The troubles of the world will not be taken from thee, viz., the bearing of children, and nursing, and, hardest of all, the loss of reward [hereafter].

38. So then he that giveth her in marriage doeth well; but he that giveth her not in marriage doeth better.

giveth her.—He manifests here the difference between marriage and celibacy; for when of marriage it is said (*v.* 36) "he sinneth not," of the celibate he says, "he doeth well:" but when he says of marriage, "he doeth well," he says of celibacy, "he doeth better."

CHAP. VIII.

12. But when ye sin so against the brethren, and wound their weak conscience, ye sin against Christ.

against Christ.—Since Christ died for the feeble ones, and they are members of Christ, the sin committed against them is committed against Christ.[1]

CHAP. IX.

2. The seal of mine apostleship are ye in the Lord.

seal.—Am I an Apostle, O people? Look thou at the Corinthians and Gentiles: have they not become believers? That result was due to an Apostle's labour, and it was I who preached to them.

---

12. [1] "The Vision of St. Molling," a religious fiction which is as old as the ninth century, is founded on this thought. When the devil appears to the saint as a royal youth, and assures him he is Christ, Molling refuses to believe it, because "when Christ used to come to converse with the servants of God, it was not in purple or royal raiment He came, but in the forms of the sick and the lepers." (Book of Leinster, p. 204, b. 1.)

5. Have we not power to lead about a sister, a wife,[1] as well as other apostles, and as the brethren of the Lord, and Cephas?

> *a sister.*—These are the women who attend on us, and are not for any other purpose.[2]

9. For it is written in the law of Moses, Thou shalt not muzzle the mouth of the ox that treadeth out the corn. Doth God take care for oxen?

> *oxen.*—The law says it not of the natural ox, but of us preachers, for we are the oxen[3] that plough the hearts of men.

13. Do ye not know that they which minister about holy things[4] live of the things of the temple? and they which wait at the altar are partakers with the altar?

> *holy things* (or, *place*).—The place in which the chief priests used to pray within the Holy of Holies.
>
> *eat.*—It was the priest's right in the temple. To them it was assigned.
>
> *serve.*—There were Levites besides who attended to the offerings.
>
> *partake.*—Part of the victim was to be burnt on the altar, and another part eaten by them; for it was appointed for their sustenance.

16. For though I preach the gospel, I have nothing to glory of: for necessity is laid upon me; yea, woe is unto me, if I preach not the gospel!

> *to glory of.*—If I preach for pay, that is, for my raiment and my sustenance, I shall not have a reward for it [hereafter].

---

5. [1] A woman—a sister.—Rh. V.

5. [2] In the ancient catalogue of the Three Orders of Irish Saints, published by Archbishop Ussher, it is said of the First Order, who flourished from the time of St. Patrick to 544, that "they rejected not the services and society of women, because, founded on the Rock Christ, they feared not the blast of temptation." The Second Order, however, who succeeded them, "refused the services of women, separating them from their monasteries." (Ussher, Vol. VI., p. 477.)

9. [3] So in the Hymn of Secundinus: "He [Patrick] ploughs their hearts and minds with the Holy Spirit."—Stanza V.

13. [4] In the holy place.—Rh. V.

1 Corinthians.

necessity.—[Yet] it is necessary for me to preach for my raiment and my sustenance; unless I preach I shall perish of cold and hunger.

woe is unto me.—" If thou shalt not warn the wicked of his way" (Ezek. xxxiii. 9): or, I shall die of cold and hunger if I preach not.

20. Unto the Jews I became a Jew.

a Jew.—By circumcising a disciple (Acts xvi. 3); that is, I became apparently a Jew.

27. I keep under my body, and bring it into subjection; lest that by any means, when I have preached to others, I myself should be a castaway.

keep under.—Through preaching, and not accepting pay.

subjection.—To preaching; or, to God and the fulfilling of the precepts of the Gospel.

a castaway.—Not practising what I preach.

CHAP. X.

4. And did all drink of the same spiritual drink: for they drank of that spiritual Rock that followed them: and that Rock was Christ.

Rock.—The rock followed them [through the desert]: or, the waters followed the sand: or, it is Christ who was born after. Question: Why is the rock [called] spiritual? The answer is not difficult; it is because it is a figure of Christ, who is the corner-stone. This is the mystical rock which poured forth the great river of spiritual doctrine which slaked the thirst of the spiritual Israel of the saints in the desert of Life when they were seeking the promised land of the living.

15. I speak as to wise men: judge ye what I say.

wise men.—It is the custom of good teachers to praise the understanding of their hearers, that they may be favourably disposed to what they hear.

27. If any of them that believe not bid you to a feast, and ye be disposed to go, whatsoever is set before you eat, asking no question for conscience sake.

> *to go.*—If you see any advantage in going; that is, any advantage in bringing the other to the faith.

30. For if I by grace be a partaker, why am I evil spoken of for that for which I give thanks?

> *by grace.*—If I have the Holy Spirit, and I give no cause to speak evil of me; that is, if my action is the result of strong faith.

CHAP. XI.

1. Be ye followers of me, even as I also am of Christ.

> *of me.*—Lest it might be too much for them to imitate Christ at once.

5. But every woman that prayeth or prophesieth with her head uncovered, dishonoureth her head: for that is even all one as if she were shaven.

> *prophesieth.*—Who preaches to her children: or to her household: or to other women.
> *head uncovered.*—It was the custom to cover their heads during prayers or preaching; or, uncovered means not wearing a crown.[1]
> *dishonoureth her head.*—That is, her husband, for it is a sign of violation of the marriage bond.
> *as if she were shaven.*—That is, deprived of her husband: or of her hair.

---

5. [1] Chrysostom mentions the custom of crowning the bride and bridegroom with garlands, which prevailed in the Greek Church. "Crowns are put upon their heads as symbols of victory, because being invincible they entered the bride-chamber without ever having been subdued by any unlawful pleasure." (IX. Homily on 1 Timothy.) The crown was therefore an evidence of purity, as the absence of it was of the contrary. The custom appears to be still observed in the East.

18. First of all, when ye come together in the church, I hear that there be divisions among you; and I partly believe it.

> *partly believe it.*—Part of it is true: or, there is a part of you contentious: or, it is as to part of the faith you are contentious.

27. Wherefore whosoever shall eat this bread, and drink this cup of the Lord, unworthily, shall be guilty of the body and blood of the Lord.

> *guilty.*—He threatens those severely, as Gregory [the Great] says, who take it unworthily, "lest they should think the Lord's body was common bread." It is crucifying Christ afresh when one goes to the body of Christ unworthily.

CHAP. XII.

6. There are diversities of operations, but it is the same God which worketh all in all.

> *same God.*—He gives three names[1] here to the Spirit (*vv.* 4, 5, 6): viz., Spirit, and Lord, and God; it is shewn here that the work is wrought by no one but the Spirit.

9. To another faith by the same Spirit; to another the gifts of healing by the same Spirit.

> *gifts of healing.*—That he may attend to (or cure) the sick, as physicians do (Pelagius): or, it means performing miracles of healing.

10. To another the working of miracles; to another prophecy; to another discerning of spirits; to another divers kinds of tongues; to another the interpretation of tongues.

> *tongues.*—Translating from one language into another, like Jerome[2] and the seventy[3] interpreters: or, to draw forth hidden meanings from single words,[4] and then to preach from them afterwards, as is the custom of preachers.

---

6. [1] Hæc tria nomina id est Spiritus et Dominus et Deus Spiritui Sancto conveniunt qui gratis et non merito cuncta spirando ac servus ministrat et potentialiter quasi Deus perficit. (Sedulius Scotus.)

10. [2] To whom we are indebted for the Vulgate. [3] The authors of the Greek translation of the Old Testament. [4] Literally, single sounds.

12. For as the body is one, and hath many members, and all the members of that one body being many are one body: so also is Christ.
   body is one.—Christ deems the saints and the just one body. This is a simile: he means, as every member serves the other in the body, so let the talent of every one of us be of service to the other, for we are one body in Christ.

13. For by one Spirit are we all baptized unto one body.
   body.—We have been massed into one body by baptism.

15. If the foot shall say, Because I am not the hand, I am not of the body; is it therefore not of the body?
   of the body.—If the foot is in the Church, this means the practical people; and the hand, this is also the practical people, who are [therefore] more[1] than others.

16. If the ear shall say, Because I am not the eye, I am not of the body; is it therefore not of the body?
   the eye.—The contemplative people.
   because I am not.—The field which the eye takes in is more delightful than I am.

21. The eye cannot say unto the hand, I have no need of thee.
   eye.—The man of contemplative life, addressing the man of practical life.

22. Nay, much more those members of the body which seem to be more feeble are necessary.
   necessary.—It is not the same degree in which one member [just referred to] can dispense with another, but much more.
   feeble.—These are the weaker; such as the heart, and liver, and other internal organs.

---

15. [1] As there are two hands and two feet.

23. And those members of the body which we think to be less honourable, upon these we bestow more abundant honour.

honour.—Through the service of the other members to them, in gathering raiment around them, and providing food for them.

24. For our comely parts have no need.

comely parts.—As the face, the hands, and the feet.

28. And God hath set some in the church, first apostles, secondarily prophets, thirdly teachers, after that miracles,[1] then gifts of healings, helps, governments, diversities of tongues.

apostles.—These have precedence, because they saw what the prophets[2] foretold.

miracles (or, *powers*).—The doers of various works: or, the performers of miracles.

helps.—Those who help in teaching and prayer: or in almsgiving.

governments.—Superiors: or vice-abbots.

30. Have all the gifts of healing? do all speak with tongues? do all interpret?

interpret.—All are not excellent at translating from one language into another: or in disputing as to sounds: or in extracting mysteries from them.

CHAP. XIII.

1. Though I speak with the tongues of men and of angels, and have not charity, I am become as sounding brass, or a tinkling cymbal.

charity.—A suitable love for God.

sounding brass.—That is, devotion without charity.

---

28. [1] *Virtues*, powers.—R.V., margin.
28. [2] Matt. xiii. 17.

2. Though I have the gift of prophecy, and understand all mysteries, and all knowledge; and though I have all faith, so that I could remove mountains, and have not charity, I am nothing.

prophecy.—The grace of preaching.
knowledge.—Of what has been done, and will be done.

9. For we know in part, and we prophesy in part.

know.—We know little of the mysteries of God.[1]
prophesy.—We preach little of the mysteries of God, for we know them not.

12. For now we see through a glass, darkly; but then face to face: now I know in part, but then shall I know even as also I am known.

in part.—It is only a part of the Godhead that I know: or, there is a part in me that knows the Godhead; that is, the soul only knows Him.
am known.—That will be wholly, and not merely in part.
darkly.—As long as we are in the body, we see the divine mysteries just as one sees something through a shadow.

13. Now abideth faith, hope, charity, these three; but the greatest of these is charity.

greatest.—Even in the present life.

CHAP. XIV.

1. Follow after charity, and desire spiritual gifts, but rather that ye may prophesy.

gifts.—The three things mentioned above, viz., faith, hope, charity.
prophesy.—That you may teach.

6. What shall I profit you, except I shall speak to you either by revelation, or by knowledge, or by prophesying, or by doctrine?[2]

prophesying.—That is, preaching; the stirring up of every one to belief, that he may be ready for baptism.
doctrine (or, *teaching*).—Teaching every one after his baptism.

---

9. [1] This thought is expanded in Bishop Butler's Sermon (No. XV.), "Upon the Ignorance of Man."
6. [2] Teaching.—R.V.

8. For if the trumpet give an uncertain sound, who shall prepare himself to the battle?

trumpet.—This is another simile—that of a trumpet, which has many different sounds. One is used for battle, another for unyoking, or for marching, or for sleep, or for council. Unless the man who sounds [the call] distinguishes, that is, if he produces only one note, the object of the call is not understood. So likewise, unless the foreign language is distinguished and translated, no one who hears it understands.

18. I thank my God I speak with more tongues than ye all.

more tongues.—He says this lest they might suppose that speaking many tongues is not a grace of the Spirit.

21. In the law it is written, With men of other tongues and other lips will I speak unto this people.

other tongues.—They (the Jews) will know every language when they shall be carried into captivity.

22. Therefore tongues are for a sign, not to them that believe, but to them that believe not.

sign.—The only advantage from the bestowing of many tongues is, that God may be magnified by it, and that unbelievers might become more ready to believe.

25. He will worship God, and report that God is in you of a truth.

God is in you.—That every one of these men is a prophet.

26. How is it, then, brethren? When ye come together, every one of you hath a psalm, hath a doctrine, hath a tongue, hath a revelation, hath an interpretation. Let all things be done unto edifying.

how is it?—What, then, is to be done in that matter? It is not hard to say. Let every one sing his psalms, and teach, and set forth. Let every one use his gift to edification.

a revelation.—Memory,[1] that is, the revealing of mysteries.

hath a psalm.—Understands the psalm, Pelagius says: That is, understands what the psalm contains.

31. For ye may all prophesy one by one, that all may learn, and all may be comforted.

> *one by one.*—This is an answer to their thoughts if, when he says, "Ye may all prophesy," anyone should say, "Then everyone will be a preacher there." For the way in which it should be done is "one by one." Question: Then what will the women do? Will they preach? No, says Paul, let them keep silence (*v.* 34).

32. And the spirits of the prophets are subject to the prophets.

> *prophets.*—Some say that the Holy Spirit, who was in the prophets of the Old Testament, was subjected to the prophets of the New, that is, to the apostles. But this is not true; for it is not of prophets he treats here, but of preachers.

36. What? came the word of God out from you? or came it unto you only?

> *unto you.*—Is it to you only it has been preached? Certainly not, but to all nations. It is not right to make anything profound of the Gospel.

CHAP. XV.

3. For I delivered unto you first of all that which I also received, how that Christ died for our sins according to the scriptures.

> *delivered to you.*—As it has been foretold in the prophets, and figured in the law, and has been declared in the Gospel.

---

26. [1] See Appendix.

1 Corinthians.

5. And that he was seen of Cephas, then of the twelve.[1]

twelve (or, *eleven*).—The eleven apostles in the supper room at Zion.

6. After that he was seen of above five hundred brethren at once; of whom the greater part remain unto this present, but some are fallen asleep.

remain.—*i.e.*, alive; if you wish to converse with any of them, you can do so.

9. For I am the least of the apostles, that am not meet to be called an apostle, because I persecuted the church of God.

meet.—For the apostleship is a great honour; it is an embassy to you from Jesus.

23. But every man in his own order: Christ the firstfruits; afterward they that are Christ's at his coming.

in his own order.—Will rise: he does not distinguish the order of time here, for all the dead will rise together.

order.—The order of reception of reward by the righteous,[2] and the order of reception of punishment by the wicked.

24. Then cometh the end, when he shall have delivered up the kingdom to God, even the Father; when he shall have put down all rule and all authority and power.

authority and power.—These were ancient names of demons,[3] for every grade of them has sinned.

26. The last enemy that shall be destroyed is death.

death.—Whatever death this may be, whether separation of body and soul: or penal death.

---

5. [1] Eleven.—Rh. V.
23. [2] Temporis, vel honoris (Pelagius and Primasius). Here the gloss rejects the former part of the note.
24. [3] Potestas, Virtus, were names assigned in the middle ages to angels of the second order of the sacred hierarchy. See Migne, Lexicon Manuale.

29. Else what shall they do which are baptized for the dead, if the dead rise not at all? Why are they then baptized for the dead?

for the dead.—For sinners who cause death: or, for those who are dead as to their wills.

32. If after the manner of men I have fought with beasts[1] at Ephesus, what advantageth it me if the dead rise not? Let us eat and drink, for to-morrow we die.

If the dead rise not.—If it is only the humanity of Christ I believe in, and I do not believe in His resurrection nor my own resurrection, *i.e.*, if the present life is all that I have.

eat and drink.—If it is thus we are, we resemble the quadruped,[2] of whom Isaiah uttered this saying.

33. Be not deceived: evil communications corrupt good manners.

manners.—Menander, the comic poet, was the author of this text; he was a Corinthian (Athenian) poet.

40. There are also celestial bodies, and bodies terrestrial: but the glory of the celestial is one, and the glory of the terrestrial is another.

glory.—He points out three things here: the difference between celestial and terrestrial bodies; the difference between celestial bodies among themselves; and the difference between terrestrial bodies among themselves. The difference between celestial bodies signifies the difference in glory between the saints in heaven. The difference between terrestrial bodies signifies the difference of the punishments inflicted on sinners in hell.

---

32. [1] (Gloss) "fierce men."
32. [2] See Isaiah xxii. 13.

43. It is sown in dishonour; it is raised in glory: it is sown in weakness; it is raised in power.

power.—There are three things here: glory, power, spirituality: these do not belong to the bodies of sinners, but to the righteous.

dishonour.—The baseness of being mingled with mould.

44. It is sown a natural body; it is raised a spiritual body.

Natural.—Animate, *i.e.*, heavy.[1]

45. The first man Adam was made a living soul: the last Adam was made a quickening spirit.

soul.—The soul was alive only: the spirit now gives life to the body [also].

47. The first man is of the earth, earthy: the second man is the Lord from heaven.

earthy.—Like his mother (the earth) was the son (Adam); [but] like his father (God) was this son (Christ).

49. As we have borne the image of the earthy, we shall[2] also bear the image of the heavenly.

shall bear (or, *let us bear*).—Let us, following the works of Christ in righteousness, use the same diligence as we did in following the deeds of Adam in sin, and then we shall be heavenly.

51. Behold, I show you a mystery: we shall not[3] all sleep, but we shall all be changed.

shall (or, *shall not*).—For though there is [in a sense] a change to sinners, he does not reckon it as a change, for they only pass from [temporal] death to [eternal] death; but the change of the just is from death to life, and this he reckons a [true] change.

---

44. [1] In the legend, *Da brón flatha nime*, the "Two Sorrows of the Kingdom of Heaven," Enoch and Elijah are said to have been sorrowful because, when in heaven, they were unable to move as swiftly as the angels, owing to the heaviness of their bodies.—*Book of Leinster*, p. 280 a.

49. [2] Let us bear.—R.V., margin.

51. [3] We shall indeed rise again; but we shall not all be changed.—Rh. V.

52. In a moment, in the twinkling of an eye, at the last trump: for the trumpet shall sound, and the dead shall be raised incorruptible, and we shall be changed.

> *last trump.*—At the last blast, for there shall be no call of assembly after that: or, at the last preaching: or, at the voice of the archangel.[1]

55. O death, where is thy sting? O grave, where is thy victory?

> *sting.*—Wherewith thou didst strike the life of all men.

56. The sting of death is sin; and the strength of sin is the law.

> *the law.*—Because it was through transgression of the law that sin has been manifested: or, the law of concupiscence, which is in every one's members, leading to the desire to sin. Every one has trangressed that law since Adam.[2]

57. But thanks be to God, which giveth us the victory through our Lord Jesus Christ.

> *victory.*—Through faith in Jesus Christ.

---

52. [1] He calls that angel a "trumpet," by whom all are summoned to "arise." Swete's Theodore, of Mopsuestia, Vol. II., p. 30.
56. [2] Ephes. ii. 3, note.

2 CORINTHIANS.

CHAP. I.

1. Paul, an apostle of Jesus Christ by the will of God, and Timothy our brother, unto the church of God which is at Corinth, with all the saints which are in all Achaia.

   apostle.—To establish his apostolic authority, he puts his own name at the beginning of the epistle.

   brother.—Timothy was their preacher and teacher, and a brother in the faith: it was not impossible that he may have been also a brother in the flesh.[1]

4. Who comforteth us in all our tribulation.

   tribulation.—Both the trials of the present life and the [apprehension of] future punishment.

5. For as the sufferings of Christ abound in us, so our consolation also aboundeth by Christ.

   consolation.—In the same degree as suffering is meted out to us, so is consolation also. God does not send suffering we cannot endure; and even for the sufferings we do endure, He gives us consolation.

9. But we had the sentence[2] of death in ourselves, that we should not trust in ourselves, but in God which raiseth the dead.

   death.—Of our nearness to death.

   sentence (or, *answer*).—We had the death of Christ for [a subject of] preaching; or, we were ready to suffer death for Christ; or [we had] tidings from death.

   Another interpretation is: life was a burthen to us. Question: What did we do? The reply is not difficult. We had the answer of death, that is, to pray urgently for our death, but we have not found it.

---

1. [1] As Timothy's father was a Greek. Acts xvi. 1, 3.
9. [2] Answer of death.—R.V. and Rh. V.

15. And in this confidence I was minded to come unto you before, that ye might have a second benefit.[1]

> *benefit* (or, *grace*).—*i.e.*, penitence. Question: What is first grace? The answer is not difficult. The grace of forgiveness of sins through baptism. The second grace is the forgiveness of sins through repentance.

19. For the Son of God, Jesus Christ, who was preached among you by us, even by me and Silvanus and Timotheus, was not yea and nay, but in him was yea.

> *yea.*—It is difficult for us to speak falsehood, for He who speaks in us, *i.e.*, Jesus Christ, is the Just One. There was not in Jesus Christ yea and nay, that is, the true and false, but in Him there is yea only, that is, the true, even everlasting righteousness.

23. Moreover, I call God for a record upon my soul, that to spare you I came not as yet unto Corinth.

> *spare you.*—Sparing you I came not to you at once to inflict vengeance and reprimand you, though I had power to do so, as Peter in the case of Ananias and Sapphira (Acts v. 1-10).

CHAP. II.

1. But I determined this with myself, that I would not come again to you in heaviness.

> *heaviness.*—That it was not necessary to blame you on this occasion. In the former Epistle he rebuked them, and shewed them their sins; in this latter he forgives and comforts them.
>
> *come.*—The arrival of the Epistle he considers as his own coming.

15. For we are unto God a sweet savour of Christ, in them that are saved, and in them that perish.

> *savour.*—Because we inspire in each other the knowledge of Christ.

---

15. [1] Grace.—R.V. and Rh. V.

saved.—Through the knowledge of the faith.

perish.—They do not savour of the faith [preached] by us, and [yet] it is preached to them in every way.

17. For we are not as many, which corrupt the word of God: but as of sincerity, but as of God, in the sight of God speak we in Christ.

speak we.—It is Christ we preach.

CHAP. III.

3. Ye are manifestly declared to be the epistle of Christ ministered by us.

epistle.—Because you fulfil the commands of Christ, while Christ is in your hearts.

6. The letter killeth, but the spirit giveth life.

killeth.—In that it avenges every one's sin on him, and there is future punishment for transgressing it. He says the letter killeth, because its burthen was "let him die the death." (Matt. xv. 4.)

13. And not as Moses, which put a vail over his face, that the children of Israel could not steadfastly look to the end of that which is abolished.

vail.—To signify that the children of Israel did not understand the mysteries [of the law], and that there was a vail of unbelief between their hearts [and him].

14. But their minds were blinded; for until this day remaineth the same vail untaken away in the reading of the old testament; which vail is done away in Christ.

day.—The day of the writing of this book (epistle).

vail.—Because they believed not in Christ as He was prefigured in the mysteries of the law.

untaken away.—From us, for there is no vail [to take away] between us and Christ; or, from those Jews, for they understood not, inasmuch as it is done away in Christ: for the vail of the letter was done away by faith in Christ. Question: What has been done with respect to them? The answer is not difficult: "Until this day remaineth the same vail," &c.

16. Nevertheless when it[1] shall turn to the Lord, the vail shall be taken away.

> *when it.*—When Israel. Twelve thousand of them [out of each tribe] shall believe.[2] Or, as many of them as believe shall understand the mysteries of the law.

17. Now the Lord is that Spirit: and where the Spirit of the Lord is, there is liberty.

> *that Spirit.*—As though he had said the Jews trust only to what is corporeal and physical. But the Lord is a spiritual Being, and all the new covenant is spiritual also.
>
> *liberty.*—Freedom from serving the law.

18. But we all, with open face beholding as in a glass the glory of the Lord, are changed into the same image from glory to glory, even as by the Spirit of the Lord.

> *image.*—[We become] like Christ in our manner of life: or, it refers to the image of the Transfiguration on Mount Tabor.

CHAP. IV.

3. But if our gospel be hid, it is hid to them that are lost.

> *hid.*—If our Gospel is dark to any one, it is not to those who fulfil it, but to those who do not believe it.[3]

4. In whom the god of this world hath blinded the minds of them which believe not, lest the light of the glorious gospel of Christ,[4] who is the image of God, should shine unto them.

> *glorious Gospel.*—In which is preached the glory of Christ.
>
> *image.*—His natural form according to His Divinity.

6. For God, who commanded the light to shine out of darkness, hath shined in our hearts, to give the light of the knowledge of the glory of God in the face of Jesus Christ.

---

16. [1] When a man.—R.V., margin.   16. [2] Revelation vii. 5-8.
3. [3] See John vii. 17.   4. [4] The Gospel of the glory of Christ.—R.V. and Rh.V.

hath shined.—It is for this reason we preach to you.

light.—The fire[1] of the Holy Ghost, by which we are skilled in the mysteries of God.

CHAP. V.

2. In this we groan, earnestly desiring to be clothed upon with our house which is from heaven.

groan.—In the body: or, wearisome to us is the separation of the body and soul.

clothed upon.—That an immortal house should be let down around us from heaven.

8. We are confident, I say, and willing rather to be absent from the body, and to be present with the Lord.

absent.—We prefer[2] to part from our bodies, if what we desired is exceedingly difficult; that is, to go to heaven in our bodies.

13. For whether we be beside ourselves, it is to God.

beside ourselves.—From charity (love); that is, from meditating on God.

14. For the love of Christ constraineth us; because we thus judge, that if one died for all, then were all dead.

constraineth us.—To be beside ourselves; or, not to think of the wishes and desires of the world, but that we should all be at one time meditating on God; at another, preaching for the love of God; both those things we do.

---

6. [1] So the *Veni, Creator Spiritus*:—

Come, Holy Ghost, our souls inspire,
And lighten with celestial fire;
Thou the anointing Spirit art,
Who dost thy seven-fold gifts impart.

8. [2] Literally, we deem it easier.

16. Wherefore henceforth know we no man after the flesh: yea, though we have known Christ after the flesh, yet henceforth know we him no more.

after the flesh.—Since Christ accomplished all these things for us, it is not right for any one to yield to the desires of the flesh: or, we know of no Christ[1] who died again for sinners.

no more.—For He has risen and ascended.

20. Now then we are ambassadors for Christ, as though God did beseech you by us: we pray you in Christ's stead, be ye reconciled to God.

ambassadors.—[We are on] an embassy, according to the words, "As my Father sent me, even so send I you." (John xx. 21.)

21. For he hath made him to be sin for us, who knew no sin; that we might be made the righteousness of God in him.

sin.—That is a [sin-]offering; for they gave the name of sin to the offering that was made for sin. For the sin of Adam's seed, therefore, was this offering made, so that it is rightly termed "sin."

CHAP. VI.

2. For he saith, I have heard thee in a time accepted, and in the day of salvation have I succoured thee: behold, now is the accepted time; behold, now is the day of salvation.

time.—The time of the New Testament: or, the lifetime of every one.

accepted time.—The time of the acceptance of faith by all, and the acceptance of all by God.

salvation.—The salvation of all by faith.

4. But in all things approving ourselves as the ministers of God, in much patience, in afflictions, in necessities, in distresses.

distresses.—Distress of mind: or, hunger and cold.

---

16. [1] Neminem novimus Christum.

5. In stripes, in imprisonments, in tumults, in labours, in watchings, in fastings.

>   *labours.*—Up to this he enumerates compulsory sufferings; he then refers to voluntary trials.

7. By the word of truth, by the power of God, by the armour of righteousness on the right hand and on the left.[1]

>   *left hand.*—That pride may not take possession of us in prosperity, nor despair in adversity.

10. As sorrowful, yet alway rejoicing: as poor, yet making many rich; as having nothing, and yet possessing all things.

>   *all things.*—All spiritual mysteries: or, all food from our own labour, that we may not suffer hunger or cold, according to the saying, "The whole world belongs to the faithful man."[2]

CHAP. VII.

1. Having therefore these promises, dearly beloved, let us cleanse ourselves from all filthiness of the flesh and spirit, perfecting holiness in the fear of God.

>   *beloved.*—He describes them by three names here [and in chap. vi.], *i.e.*, the temple of God, his sons, and his dearly-loved ones.
>
>   *ourselves.*—He joins himself with them, as is the custom of good teachers.

10. For godly sorrow worketh repentance to salvation not to be repented of: but the sorrow of the world worketh death.

>   *sorrow of the world.*—About the cares of the world; sorrow for anything that has perished, and for anything unattainable, and for anything that another has, and you have not.

---

7. [1] For the figurative use of the words "right and left," compare *dextra auspicia prospera*, Festus, and *sinister = adversus.*—Vergil, Georg. I. 444.
10. [2] See 1 Cor. iii. 21.

CHAP. VIII.

20. Avoiding this, that no man should blame us in this abundance which is administered by us.

blame us.—For appropriating alms: or, the suspicion that the collection they brought would not be sent to Jerusalem: or, the taking of pay for our preaching. As I do not receive [any], neither does Luke.

23. They are the messengers of the churches, and the glory[1] of Christ.

glory.—They preach the glory of God in all the churches.

CHAP. IX.

1. For as touching the ministering to the saints, it is superfluous for me to write to you.

ministering.—Two things are treated of in the following passage: It is the preaching of morality to all the Corinthians. I do not speak to you, he says, of the alms which are taken to Jerusalem, for I know you are ready to give. Or, it refers to the alms he had suggested before; but it is on account of the laity he refers to them now; as for ecclesiastics and perfect ones, there was no need to remind them.

CHAP. X.

7. If any man trust to himself that he is Christ's, let him of himself think this again, that, as he is Christ's, even so are we Christ's.

Christ's.—As he had just boasted that he had power, he declares now that he is a servant, and not the lord; and having then said he is a servant, he reflects again that he should perform the work of servant; but let not any one suppose that he is no more than a servant; and that even when we boasted it was not for love of boasting, but for your advantage, so that you might believe, and be imitators of my example, and might not believe in any one who could not do these works.

---

23. [1] *In gloria Christi.* In the glory of Christ.

10. His letters, say they, are weighty and powerful; but his bodily presence is weak, and his speech contemptible.

speech.—His discourse is not eloquent; that is, it is not powerful, but it is simple and clear.

letters.—Important are the judgments which are written in his epistles.

CHAP. XI.

1. Would to God ye could bear with me a little in my folly: and indeed bear with me.

bear.—You bear with one who is worse to you, viz., the false apostle.

2. That I may present you as a chaste virgin to Christ.

virgin.—Who does not think of any one else but Christ.

3. For I fear, lest by any means, as the serpent beguiled Eve through his subtilty, so your minds should be corrupted from the simplicity that is in Christ.

corrupted.—It was to Eve the serpent went first, and not to Adam, for the woman is weaker than the man. I am not surprised then that you should be treated as weak people.

14. And no marvel; for Satan himself is transformed into an angel of light.

Satan.—He begins to claim even equality[1] with God.

24. Of the Jews five times received I forty stripes save one.

forty.—Save one; that is, one thong was wanting to it when it struck, and thus it was "save one:" or, it is the blows themselves, that is, forty blows, less one, *i.e.*, not together, but each separately, five forties of blows: or, a special kind of scourge wherein there were forty thongs.

14.' [1] See Isaiah xiv. 14.

27. In hunger and thirst, in fastings often.

fastings.—*i.e.*, compulsory fastings.

28. Beside those things that are without, that which cometh upon me daily, the care of all the churches.

without.—Thinking of the faithful brethren.

care of all the churches.—Lest false apostles should come to them.

CHAP. XII.

6. For though I would desire to glory, I shall not be a fool: for I will say the truth, but now I forbear.

forbear.—I abase myself: or, I cut short my story, lest I should be a fool: I have not recounted all I saw, lest my hearers should honour me, *i.e.*, lest I should be considered not a man but a God.

7. There was given to me a thorn in the flesh, the messenger of Satan to buffet me, lest I should be exalted above measure.

thorn in the flesh.—Headache:[1] or persecution:[2] or fleshly appetites, according to Isidore.[3]

8. For this thing I besought the Lord thrice, that it might depart from me.

besought.—What is contrary to salvation is denied to us notwithstanding our prayers for it.

11. In nothing am I behind the very chiefest apostles, though I be nothing.

chiefest.—Those who were in the presence of Christ.

---

7. [1] Quidam enim dicunt eum frequenter dolore capitis laborasse. (Pelagius.)
7. [2] Stimulum carnis angelum Satanæ tentationes persecutionum Apostolus se sustinuisse significat. (Pelagius.)
7. [3] Isidorus Hispalensis, or Isidore of Seville, who flourished A.D. 595.

2 Corinthians.

CHAP. XIII.

2. I told you before, and foretell you, as if I were present the second time.

present.—He is present when his epistle is read.

4. We also are weak in[1] him, but we shall live with him by the power of God toward you.

weak in him (or, *with him*).—We bear the likeness of His human nature.

5. Know ye not your own selves, how that Jesus Christ is in you, except ye be reprobates?

reprobates.—Unless you practise what was preached to you.

14. The grace of the Lord Jesus Christ, and the love of God, and the communion of the Holy Ghost be with you all.

grace.—Of the remission of sins.
love of God.—God's love to you, and your love to God.
communion.—So that the Holy Ghost may be in you.
with you.—Let it be given to you all.

GALATIANS.

CHAP. I.

1. Paul, an apostle (not of men, neither by man, but by Jesus Christ, and God the Father, who raised him from the dead).

of men.—Not by any men, says Pelagius; that is, not from James or John; he is not an apostle of an apostle.

5. To whom be glory for ever and ever.

glory.—To him glory should be given, and not to men nor to [the] elements.

---

4. [1] With him.—R.V.

7. Which is not another [gospel]; but there be some that trouble you, and would pervert the gospel of Christ.

> *another.*—There is no other ground on which ye should disseminate the Gospel (or upon which the Gospel is published)[1] but Christ, for it is He who was prefigured in the law, and announced in the Gospel.
>
> *pervert.*—They use the Gospel to confirm the Old Testament; but it would be more suitable that [the Old Testament], *i.e.*, the figure, should confirm the truth,[2] that is the New Testament.

8. But though we, or an angel from heaven, preach any other gospel unto you than that which we have preached unto you, let him be accursed.

> *an angel.*—It is not right for you to listen to it; that is, though one of the angels of heaven preach to you, do not believe him, nor any of the apostles, unless it is the same doctrine as we preach. You will learn no good by listening to them, for their end will be *anathema*.

13. For ye have heard of my conversation in time past in the Jews' religion.

> *conversation.*—He speaks of his conversation (or manner of life), not of his grace, says St Jerome [as though he would say] I was not a good man originally.

14. Being more exceedingly zealous for the traditions[3] of my fathers.

> *zealous.*—To contend for the rule.

---

7. [1] Ni fil folad naill fora sernte, *de qua celebretur evangelium.*—Zeuss, 913*b*.
7. [2] Compare John i. 17.
14. [3] It is doubtful whether the law of Moses is included in this expression. (Lightfoot.) And accordingly the gloss avoids the use of the word for *law*.

17. Neither went I up to Jerusalem to them which were apostles before me; but I went into Arabia, and returned again unto Damascus.

returned.—To preach[1] the Gospel; the reason he mentions this is that the false apostles said he was a disciple of the apostles.

CHAP. II.

1. Fourteen years after I went up again to Jerusalem with Barnabas, and took Titus with me also.

fourteen.—It was not in my boyhood I returned.

Barnabas.—Barnabas was a Jew; Titus a Gentile; these two know that it was not to study [theology] I went there. They are disciples of Jesus, and were elected at the same time to the apostleship of the Gentiles.

2. I communicated unto them that gospel which I preach among the Gentiles, but privately to them which were of reputation.

communicated.—I told them, that is, I declared it to them, if perchance there may have been anything erroneous in it, and [it appeared that] there was not.

3-4. But neither Titus, who was with me, being a Greek, was compelled to be circumcised;[2] and that[3] because of false brethren.

circumcised.—Two senses are admissible here, either that Titus was circumcised or not. The latter is the true sense, for we read, "Neither was he compelled to be circumcised." Timothy was circumcised, but Titus[4] was not.

---

17. [1] Non quod mihi necesse fuit ut ab illis aliquid edocerer: sed de Damasco in Arabiam protinus ibam ut docerem quod mihi a Deo revelatum fuerat. (Pelagius.) So also Theodore of Mopsuestia.

3-4. [2] Non didici sed contuli Evangelium per quod gentes sola fide salvantur. (Pelagius.) Non didici ab illis sed contuli cum illis. (Primasius.)

3-4. [3] But it was because of.—R.V., margin and Rh. V.

3-4. [4] Here the writer of the gloss deserts Pelagius, who maintained that Titus was circumcised. Reddit causas cur circumcidit Titum; non quia illi circumcisio prodesset, sed ut scandalum imminens vitaretur. (Pelagius.) Hilary maintained that he was not.

6. But of these who seemed to be somewhat, (whatsoever they were, it maketh no matter to me: God accepteth no man's person:) for they who seemed to be somewhat in conference added nothing to me.
> *those who seemed.*—Peter, and James, and John. Their persons are not superior to those of the other apostles, though they were prior in the faith, for God accepteth no man's person.

11. But when Peter was come to Antioch, I withstood him to the face, because he was to be blamed.
> *withstood him.*—I did not study [theology] with Peter, but I rebuked him for his agreement and connivance with the Jews: it was right to do so: this is to the praise of the sacred humility of Peter, and the zeal for righteousness of Paul.

20. I am crucified with Christ: nevertheless I live; yet not I, but Christ liveth in me.
> *crucified.*—So that I am dead to the will of the flesh, like Christ.
>
> *I live.*—I deny it; it is not I who live: that is, I am [only] alive, because Christ is in me.

CHAP. III.

6. Even as Abraham believed God, and it was accounted to him for righteousness.
> *righteousness.*—As it was faith sanctified Abraham, not the deeds of the law, it is that also that sanctified you. His faith justified him, as if he lived under the New Testament.

13. Christ hath redeemed us from the curse of the law, being made a curse for us.
> *curse.*—He was offered up, on account of sin and the curse.

CHAP. IV.

2. But is under tutors and governors until the time appointed of the father.
> *until the time.*—Until it is time for him to take the land (farm).

Galatians.   85

3. Even so we, when we were children, were in bondage under the elements of the world.

elements.—Rudiments; that is, under the commandments of the law; or, under the teachers[1] of the law.

6. And because ye are sons, God hath sent forth the Spirit of his Son into your hearts, crying, Abba, Father.

crying, Abba, Father.—For it is He who [alone] is wise as to the recognition[2] of the Father.

9. But now, after that ye have known God, or rather are known of God, how turn ye again to the weak and beggarly elements?

turn ye again.—Why does he say this, although these men were never under the law of the Old Testament? It is not difficult to say. For it is the same in his view to come under the obedience of the law and to serve idols.[3]

12. Brethren, I beseech you, be as I am; for I am as ye are; ye have not injured me at all.

as I am.—It is not difficult for you to imitate me, for "I also am a man." (Acts x. 26.)

17. They zealously affect you, but not well; yea, they would exclude you, that ye might affect them.

affect you.—The false apostles are jealous of you, or envy you.

not well.—Not for your good: not like me, who can say, "The zeal of thine house hath eaten me up." (Psalm lxix. 9.)

CHAP. V.

20. Idolatry.

idolatry.—That is covetousness.

25. If we live in the Spirit, let us also walk in the Spirit.

Spirit.—If our lives are spiritual, let our actions be so too.

---

3. [1] A few of the Fathers, Jerome, Gennadius, and Primasius, adopt the sense "elementary teaching;" this is probably the correct interpretation. (Lightfoot.)
6. [2] 1 Cor. ii. 11.
9. [3] The days and months (v. 10) were calculated by the movements of the sun and moon, and thus they might be said to observe and reverence them like the Gentiles.

CHAP. VI.

4. But let every man prove his own work, and then shall he have rejoicing in himself alone, and not in another.
every man.—He first gave orders to spiritual people that they should well instruct the unlearned; that each should bear the other's burthens; here, on the contrary, he commands that the weaker in learning should do good to their masters. (Jerome.)

8. He that soweth to his flesh shall of the flesh reap corruption.
corruption.—Everlasting punishment shall be their recompense.

9. Let us not be weary in well-doing: for in due season we shall reap, if we faint not.
if we faint not.—i.e., in faith [of the reward] of our work. Let us not cease from doing good, that we may obtain eternal life, as it is said, "He that shall endure unto the end, the same shall be saved." (Matt. xxiv. 13.)
due season.—When it is time; that is, in the Day of Judgment.

14. Our Lord Jesus Christ, by whom the world is crucified unto me, and I unto the world.
crucified unto me.—As He is dead in the grave, so each of us, I and the world, are dead to each other.

16. And as many as walk according to this rule, peace be on them, and mercy, and upon the Israel of God.
Israel.—The saints who see God,[1] and fulfil His will.

17. From henceforth let no man trouble me: for I bear in my body the marks[2] of the Lord Jesus.
marks.—The two wounds, *i.e.*, the pains from the scourges.
in my body.—The diadem (or credentials) of apostolic authority, so that I am able to administer punishment and correction to any one.

---

16. [1] The Irish divines adopted the interpretation of the name Israel mentioned by Jerome:—"Vir aut mens videns Deum." (Todd, *Liber Hymnorum*, p. 20). So in the Liturgy of St. Clement:—"The God of Israel, *i.e.*, of him that truly seeth Thee." (Neale's Primitive Liturgies, p. 92.)

17. Perhaps alluding to Acts xvi. 22; xxi. 32.

EPHESIANS.

CHAP. I.

5. Having predestinated us unto the adoption of children by Jesus Christ to himself, according to the good pleasure of his will.

adoption.—From of old we have been destined, so that we are sons by election, not by nature.

7. In whom we have redemption through his blood, the forgiveness of sins, according to the riches of his grace.

through his blood.—Through the material[1] blood which poured from His side when He was on the cross, and through the spiritual blood which is offered every day upon the altar.

12. That we should be to the praise of his glory, who first trusted[2] in Christ.

trusted (or, *hoped*).—Through [the predictions of] the prophets, that He would come to us.

13. Ye were sealed[3] with that holy Spirit of promise.

sealed (or, *signed*).—There is a sign on you, that is, the Holy Spirit; or, you are impressed with a seal.

18. The eyes of your understanding being enlightened.

enlightened.—What I pray for is, that you may understand the knowledge of God, and that the darkness of earthly desires may not be over the eye of your soul; *i.e.*, that your soul's eye may be clear."[4]

21. Far above all principality, and power, and might.

above.—He places Him above all powers in heaven and earth. According to others, he places Him above the ranks of heaven only,[5] and there is no impossibility in supposing that there is a difference amongst them, one rank being higher than another, as in earthly things.

---

7. [1] Literally, "historical."   12. [2] Hoped.—R.V. and Rh. V.
13. [3] Signed.—Rh. V.   18. [4] Matt. vi. 22, 23.   21. [5] 1 Peter iii. 22.

23. [The Church] which is his body, the fulness of him that filleth all in all.

body.—The saints and the righteous are His body. Christ is the head, and the saints are the body.

CHAP. II.

2. The spirit that now worketh in the children of disobedience.[1]

disobedience (or, *unbelief*).—As Christ works in the righteous, according to what St. Paul says: "God who worketh in you" (Phil. ii. 13), so then does the devil work in the children of unbelief. Sons, then, are these by works, not by nature. The children of unbelief or despair are they who despaired of their salvation through Christ's passion.

3. And were by nature children of wrath, even as others.

nature.—It is not by the nature of our original creation, but by our sinful nature, that we have transgressed since Adam.

7. That in the ages to come he might show the exceeding riches of his grace in his kindness toward us, through Christ Jesus.

grace.—It is His grace that saved us, and not our own merits.

10. Good works, which God hath before ordained[2] that we should walk in them.

ordained (or, *prepared*).—In three ways: He preached them; He fulfilled them; He granted them to us, that we might perform them (*i.e.*, gave us power to do so).

14. Who hath broken down the middle wall of partition between us.

wall.—So that the wall that was between God and man, that is, sin, and which was between body and soul, was broken down after the coming of Christ.

---

2. [1] Unbelief.—Rh. V.
10. [2] Prepared.- R.V. and Rh. V.

15. Having abolished in his flesh the enmity, even the law of commandments contained in ordinances.

in his flesh.—That is, while He was in the flesh.

16. That he might reconcile both unto God in one body by the cross.

body.—By bestowing the gifts of the Spirit on all.

20. Built upon the foundation of the apostles and prophets, Jesus Christ himself being the chief corner stone.

built.—The apostles and prophets came first into the building; you yourselves came afterwards. Christ, then, is the city, and the saints united to Christ are the citizens.

21. In whom all the building, fitly framed together, groweth unto an holy temple in the Lord.

temple.—The assembly of the saints; they are called a temple, because Christ dwells in them: *i.e.*, it is a habitation for God.

CHAP. III.

9. And to make all men see what is the fellowship of the mystery, which from the beginning of the world hath been hid in God, who created all things by Jesus Christ.

mystery.—Of the salvation of the human race, and of the bestowing of the Holy Spirit on them, which was hidden in the secrets of the Godhead; and even the family of heaven knew not of it until the apostles revealed it to them, that is, to the believers of the New Testament, and to the family of heaven.

10. To the intent that now unto the principalities and powers in heavenly places might be known by the church the manifold wisdom of God.

principalities and powers.—He puts these two names only for all the celestial ranks; for the family of heaven knew not the mysteries of the Incarnation until they were revealed by the apostles: as we learn from what was said [by the angels], "Who is this King of glory?" (Ps. xxiv. 8): or, the names are put for all the ranks of the Church of the New Testament, to which the apostles preached according to the expression, "Our conversation is in heaven" (Phil. iii. 20): or, it means in heavenly gifts (not places).

18, 19. May be able to comprehend with all saints what is the breadth, and length, and depth, and height; and to know the love of Christ.

comprehend.—These four are in the secrets of the Godhead, and also in the Cross[1] of Christ: or, they are the four virtues of the soul.

to know.—The knowledge is either of the incarnation, or of the divine nature of Christ. With His right hand He saved the left of the world, *i.e.*, the North; with His left hand He saved the right part of the world, *i.e.*, the South; His head redeemed the East, and His feet the West.

CHAP. IV.

5. One Lord, one faith, one baptism.

one baptism.—Though the dipping is threefold.[2]

9. That he ascended, what is it but that he also descended first into the lower parts of the earth?

what is it.—Why is it said He ascended, but because He had descended first into the lower parts of the earth?

he ascended.—Over the many spaces.[3]

12. For the perfecting of the saints, for[4] the work of the ministry, for the edifying of the body of Christ.

for (or, *unto*).—So that every one may be perfect in the works of the ministry of the Church.

edifying.—This comes to pass from many gifts in many persons.

---

18. [1] The four limbs of the Cross.
5. [2] The question whether there should be one or three immersions in baptism was a subject of controversy, particularly in Spain, in the seventh century. Single immersion lingered on in Brittany until the seventeenth century. Mr. Haddan says it is conjectured to have been a Scotch or British practice. It would appear from this gloss that it was not in use in Ireland. See on Colossians ii. 12.
9. [3] These spaces (*rée*) were described by the Irish as extending from the earth to the twelve signs of the Zodiac. (Zeuss, Gram. Celt, p. 19.)
12. [4] *Unto.*—R.V.

22. The old man, which is corrupt according to the deceitful lusts.

old man.—The mass of old sins: or, Adam with his deeds.

24. That ye put on the new man, which after God is created in righteousness and true holiness.

new man.—The mass of virtues: or, Christ with His works.

after God.—By the Holy Spirit: thereby is a man made spiritual.

26. Be ye angry, and sin not: let not the sun go down upon your wrath.

angry.—Against your sins, so that they may not continue with you.

sun go down.—That is Christ, for He does not abide in a vessel of wrath.[1]

27. Neither give place to the devil.

give place.—Let him not come into your heart[2] instead of God.

28. Let him that stole steal no more.

stole.—Let him [the devil] not snatch God from him, or him from God: or, it means theft in the literal sense.

30. Grieve not the holy Spirit of God, whereby ye are sealed unto the day of redemption.

holy Spirit.—For as man was originally made in the image of God, so he is made in the image of the Spirit now.

CHAP. V.

2. An offering and a sacrifice to God for a sweet-smelling savour.

sacrifice.—Great was His love in that He went even to the Cross for us.

---

26. [1] Ne scientiæ lumen in tua indignatione deficiat.—Pelagius. Primasius, considering this inadequate, amends it thus:—*Ne fidei vel* scientiæ lumen in tua indignatione deficiat.

27. [2] Porta enim Diaboli est peccatum.—Pelagius.

offering.—A drink-offering, by His blood.
savour.—The perfume of that offering filled the whole world and heaven.

5. Nor covetous man, who is an idolater.

idolater.—So called from the greatness of the sin, and because he serves [riches] in the same way that [idols] are served.

CHAP. VI.

13. Wherefore take unto you the whole armour of God, that ye may be able to withstand in the evil day.

armour.—Because you are engaged in a conflict: or, because you wrestle not against flesh and blood: let your armour be the armour of God, and no other.

PHILIPPIANS.

CHAP. I.

1. Paul and Timotheus, the servants of Jesus Christ, to all the saints in Christ Jesus which are at Philippi.

saints.—Those who are in the unity of Christ's body.

6. That he which hath begun a good work in you will perform it until the day of Jesus Christ.

day of Jesus Christ.—The day of the separation of soul and body: or, the day of judgment.

20. Christ shall be magnified in my body, whether it be by life, or by death.

magnified.—Through the practising and preaching of the Gospel.
body.—While I live the name of Christ shall be the subject of my preaching.

CHAP. II.

5. Let this mind be in you which was also in Christ Jesus.

> *in Christ Jesus.*—He gave not glory to Himself, but to the Father.

6. Who, being in the form of God, thought it not robbery to be equal with God.

> *equal.*—In the might and majesty of God.

11. And that every tongue should confess that Jesus Christ is Lord, to the glory of God the Father.

> *every tongue.*—It is not easy to conceal it: most of them know it [already].

25. Epaphroditus, my brother, and companion in labour, and fellowsoldier.

> *fellowsoldier.*—In fighting against the devil.

CHAP. III.

9. And be found in him, not having mine own righteousness.

> *righteousness.*—He shews here that it is the righteousness of Christ that justifies, and not the righteousness of the law.

13. This one thing I do, forgetting those things which are behind, and reaching forth unto those things which are before.

> *one thing I do.*—He compares himself to a soldier who runs for the crown of victory: it is his habit not to take count of that part of his path which is behind, but of what is before him, until he passes the goal and attains the prize: it was in that manner Paul acted, and so ought every one, viz., to be always penitent until he reaches the crown, that is, the heavenly reward.

19. Whose God is their belly.

> *God.*—That is, who preach for the sake of their food.

21. Who shall change our vile body, that it may be fashioned like unto his glorious body.

vile body.—The body which He received from us : or, our own body.

CHAP. IV.

3. Help those women which laboured with me in the gospel.

laboured.—In practising its precepts, not in preaching.

5. Let your moderation[1] be known unto all men. The Lord is at hand.

moderation (or, *gentleness*).—Be gentle to all.
the Lord is at hand.—To give you whatsoever you need.

7. The peace of God, which passeth all understanding, shall keep your hearts and minds through Christ Jesus.

peace.—It is the noblest of all feelings, but all benevolence is not the same, for it is perishable and unstable unless it is influenced by Him.

---

1 THESSALONIANS.

CHAP. I.

4. Knowing, brethren beloved, your election of God.

election.—You were called to be in the body of Christ.

5. For our gospel came not unto you in word only, but also in power, and in the Holy Ghost, and in much assurance.[2]

assurance (or, *fulness*).—In perfect righteousness of conversation and life : or, in the fulness of knowledge of the divinity and humanity of Christ.

---

5. [1] Gentleness.—R.V.
   [2] Fulness.—R.V. and Rh. V.

1 Thessalonians.

6. Ye became followers[1] of us and of the Lord, having received the word in much affliction.

> *followers* (or, *imitators*).—He deems it too high to tell them to imitate God at once, but this [eventually] is the result, though it may be slow.

10. Jesus, which delivered[2] us from the wrath to come.

> *delivered* (or, *delivereth*).—As He has saved us from sin, we are sure He will save us in the future.

CHAP. II.

7. We were gentle[3] among you, even as a nurse cherisheth her children.

> *gentle* (or, *babes*).—Question: Does he consider a babe and a nurse the same? Certainly not, [yet] they are the same [in a sense], for it is the habit of a nurse to make a weakling of herself in the teaching of her charge, for her wish is to be in a state of childhood with every babe. So, Paul says, "we were among you."

9. Labouring night and day, because we would not be chargeable unto any of you, we preached unto you.

> *labouring.*—Making ropes[4] [tents] by night to sell for food and raiment for his household; preaching by day to save the souls of many.

18. Wherefore we would have come unto you, even I Paul, once and again; but Satan hindered us.

> *hindered.*—By the tribulations arising from persecution: or, Satan means every adversary.

CHAP. IV.

14. For if we believe that Jesus died and rose again, even so them also which sleep in Jesus will God bring with him.

> *bring with Him.*—This is his answer to the heretics;[5] it is not easy to argue or abide against him.

---

6. [1] Imitators.—R.V.   10. [2] Delivereth.—R.V.
7. [3] Babes.—R.V.; little ones.—Rh. V.
9. [4] The Glosser mistook σκηναι, tents, for σχοῖναι, ropes.
14. [5] The heretics here appear to be those who held the opinions afterwards known as those of the Docetæ, viz., that Christ's body was not real flesh and blood, but only in appearance. Theodoret was of opinion that the words, "Jesus died," had reference to them.

15. For this we say unto you by the word of the Lord, that we which are alive and remain unto the coming of the Lord shall not prevent them which are asleep.

> *u e.*—He joins himself here with those whom the judgment will find alive.[1] They will die and rise again in the same hour. As swift will be their resurrection as our taking up, says Pelagius. The awakening of those who sleep will be easy. The apostle, Pelagius observes, always treats the day of judgment as to be looked for; as if it might find them in the body.

16. For the Lord himself shall descend from heaven with a shout, with the voice of the archangel, and with the trump of God: and the dead in Christ shall rise first.

> *rise.*—Sleep will not avail anyone then.
> *trump.*—With the sound which accompanied God Himself, as on Mount Sinai.
> *first.*—More noble will be their resurrection: or, they shall rise leaders[2] (or chiefs).

CHAP. V.

1. But of the times and the seasons,[3] brethren, ye have no need that I write unto you.

> *times.*—This is answer to the opinions of those who said the resurrection would be immediately.
> *seasons* (or, *moments*).—It will not be a time of a moment's duration.

17. Pray without ceasing.

> *pray.*—Question: What is prayer without ceasing? The answer is not difficult. Some say it is celebrating

---

15. [1] Pelagius succeeded in bringing out more exactly the force of ἡμεῖς, which Jerome, Theodoret, Chrysostom, and others, partly missed.—Swete, Vol. II., p. 29*n.*
16. [2] *Resurgent primi,* which admits of either meaning, though the Greek does not.
1. [3] Moments.—Rh. V.

the [Canonical] Hours,¹ but this is not the true meaning. But it is when all the members [of the body] are inclined to good deeds, and evil deeds are put away from them. Then, when doing good, they are praying to God, that is, they incline their eyes to see what is good, as Job says, " I made a covenant with mine eyes" (chap. xxxi. 1).

21. Prove all things; hold fast that which is good.
hold fast.—Every good thing he preaches, perform thou.

23. I pray God your whole spirit and soul and body be preserved blameless.
*spirit.*²—The primary part of the soul, by which we understand: or the Holy Ghost, *i.e.*, as it has been imparted to us.

27. I charge you by the Lord that this epistle be read unto all the holy brethren.
read.—That it be read out [aloud]; that no one may be ignorant of it.

28. The grace of our Lord Jesus Christ be with you [all].³
[*all*].—Without exception.

---

17. ¹ This view is attributed to St. Augustine in the gloss on the words, "sine intermissione Deum orat Dominum," in the Hymn of Secundinus (*Liber Hymnorum*, p. 22). Hilary, while stating that it is physically impossible for anyone to obey the command literally, proposed two modes of complying with it. 1. One may pray in his heart, as Moses, to whom it was said, "Why criest thou to me?" though he was silent at the time. 2. Or, let every act you perform be such that it may be a constant prayer to God for you. This appears to be the meaning of the gloss.

The opinion here ascribed to Augustine, though rejected in the ninth century by this Commentary, was accepted in the twelfth by the compilers of the Book of Hymns.

23. ² Theodore of Mopsuestia, Chrysostom, and the School of Antioch, took this to mean the Holy Spirit; but the Alexandrians regarded the verse as a witness to the threefold division of human nature. In reply to their objections, Chrysostom explains that it is the "gift" of the Spirit that is meant. The gloss thus gives the views of both, but places the Alexandrian first.

28. ³ *Omnibus*, which is not in the Vulgate.

2 THESSALONIANS.

CHAP. I.

6. Seeing it is a righteous thing with God to recompense tribulation to them that trouble you.

seeing it is.—It is certainly true.[1]
trouble you.—O ye righteous ones!

8. In flaming fire taking vengeance on them that know not God, and that obey not the gospel of our Lord Jesus Christ.

flaming fire.—It will not be like His first coming.
vengeance.—He will visit them all. He protects neither those who never heard Him, nor those who [having heard] transgress.

10. Because our testimony among[2] you was believed in that day.

believed.—You believed the doctrine we taught you about the day of judgment: or, we were entrusted to bear testimony of you in the day of judgment.

CHAP. II.

3. That day shall not come except there come a falling away first, and that man of sin be revealed, the son of perdition.

man of sin.—full of sin.[3]
a falling away.—Until the fall of the Roman Empire, that is, the departure of empire from the Romans: or, the

---

6. [1] The Latin, "si tamen," suggesting some uncertainty, the note of Pelagius is, "hic si tamen confirmantis sermo est non dubitantis." The Revised Version, however, has, "if so be that it is."
10. [2] Unto you.—R.V.
3. [3] Literally, of full sin. Compare Matthew xxiii. 32; Genesis xv. 16. Homo peccati diabolus scilicet.—Pelagius. But Primasius has, id est diaboli. Pelagius thus held that the man of sin was the devil, but Primasius that he was a devilish man. Mr. Swete says: "Theodore of Mopsuestia in regarding the Antichrist as an individual man, the peculiar instrument of Satan, follows the stream of early Christian exegesis."—ii., 50*n*. Primasius appears to agree with Theodore.

falling away of believers into unbelief : or, until the devil comes, whose names are Discessio and Refuga.¹

4. Who opposeth and exalteth himself above all that is called God, or that is worshipped; so that he as God sitteth in the temple of God, shewing himself that he is God.

sitteth.—He sits in the temple setting himself forth as Christ :² or, the temple will be rebuilt by him, and he will preach the rites of the law of the Old Testament, and will destroy the law of the New Testament.³

6. And now ye know what withholdeth⁴ that he might be revealed in his time.

withholdeth.—The destruction of the Roman Empire must first take place. You know why he delays his manifestation, even that the time which has been foretold of him may come.

7. For the mystery of iniquity doth already work : only he who now letteth will let, until he be taken out of the way.

work.— . . . The deeds which he will do after his coming, his family⁵ and his members do [now]; it is this that delays him.

will let.—While it holds the kingdom (*i.e.*, the Roman Empire).⁶

8. And then shall that Wicked be revealed, whom the Lord shall consume with the spirit of his mouth, and shall destroy with the brightness of his coming.

that wicked.—Antichrist.

brightness.—By the brightness of the divinity of Christ.

---

3. ¹ That is, Departer and Deserter. Desertio veritatis, vel sui principatus: sive discessio gentilium a Romano imperio. Discessio autem diabolus non immerito dicitur ab eo quod discessit a Deo.—Primasius, abbreviated from Pelagius.

4. ² This identification of Antichrist with a false Christ (Matt. xxiv. 24) is that of Cyril, Theodore, and others.

4. ³ Templum Hierosolymis restituet et omnia legis ceremonialia restaurabit tantum ut evangelium Christi dissolvat.—Primasius and Pelagius.

6. ⁴ Theodore of Mopsuestia and Theodoret held that τὸ κατέχον was a limit of time fixed by a divine decree.

7. ⁵ "The mystery works in those who by false doctrines smooth his way."—Pelagius.

7. ⁶ Tertullian, Jerome, Augustine, Cyril of Jerusalem, Chrysostom, Ambrose, and others, held this view.

9. Even him, whose coming is after the working of Satan with all power and signs and lying wonders.

working of Satan.—He will be opposed to God and His Gospel.

signs.—He will perform false miracles and false signs, as the Druids did through him.[1]

10. With all deceivableness of unrighteousness in them that perish; because they received not the love of the truth, that they might be saved.

received not.—No excuse will avail them in the day of judgment, when it shall be said to them, "Why did you not believe in Christ?"[2] If they reply, "We did not recognise Him, for His human nature concealed His divinity" [the answer will be], "You believed in the devil, though he [also] was incarnate." It is right, then, that they who are not admitted to the glory of Christ should share the condemnation of the devil.

16. Now our Lord Jesus Christ himself, and God, even[3] our Father, which hath loved us, and hath given us everlasting consolation[4] and good hope through grace.

even (or, *and*).—He indicates the Trinity here: the Son, when he says "our Lord;" the Father, when he says "God;" and the Holy Ghost, when he speaks of "a Comforter."

CHAP. III.

1. Finally, my brethren, pray for us, that the word of the Lord may have free course, and be glorified, even as it is with you.

free course.—In every one's heart. Pray not for anything but the success of the preaching [of the Gospel].

---

9. [1] The mention of Druids suggests the early date of this Commentary.
10. [2] Ut non se per incarnationis Christi obscuritatem excusent divinis virtutibus non credidisse cum homini diabolica arte fallenti crediderunt quia in hominis effigie apparehit.—Pelagius and Primasius. From Theodore of Mopsuestia's standpoint, the parallel between the Incarnation and the indwelling of Satan in the Man of Sin seemed all but complete.—Swete, ii. 50.
16. [3] And.—R.V.
16. [4] *Consolatio,* comfort.—R.V.

6. Withdraw yourselves from every brother that walketh disorderly.

walketh.—For the purpose of begging.[1]

COLOSSIANS.

CHAP. I.

9. That ye might be filled with the knowledge of his will in all wisdom and spiritual understanding.

wisdom.—That is, the knowledge of the Godhead.
understanding.—Knowledge of the divine mysteries.

15. Who is the image of the invisible God, the firstborn of every creature.

image.—He is the true image of the God of heaven: or, by Him God the Father is known.

20. And having made peace through the blood of his cross, by him to reconcile all things unto himself.

cross.—This is the name of the act of crucifying.

24. And fill up that which is behind of the afflictions of Christ in my flesh for his body's sake, which is the church.

fill up.—That which was lacking to me of the fulfilment of Christ's passion, I am doing, that is, undergoing martyrdom.

25. To fulfil the word of God.

word of God.—That is, the Gospel, which embraces the seven[2] things that were prophesied of Christ.

---

6. [1] The man who "walks to support himself" seems to have been as familiar a figure in the ninth century as in the nineteenth.

25. [2] The seven gifts of the Spirit, *i.e.*, wisdom, understanding, counsel, might, knowledge, fear of the Lord, and godliness.

29. Whereunto I also labour, striving according to his working, which worketh in me mightily.

> *labour.*—I am contending with Him as to imitating His deeds, and as to taking example from Him, so that I may attain equality with Him, and that He may work with me in this.

CHAP. II.

1. For you, and for them at Laodicea.

> *them.*—There are Colossians, then, in Laodicea.

4. And this I say, lest any man should beguile you with enticing words.

> *any man.*—That is, the philosophers; for no philosopher will be wiser than you will be if you are in Christ.

7. Rooted and built up in him.

> *in Him.*—In the unity of His body.

8. Beware lest any man spoil you through philosophy and vain deceit, ... not after Christ.

> *spoil you.*—Though he may be acute and eloquent in his dissertations. For it is the habit of philosophers to compose dissertations on the elements, and to discuss them, and not believe what is declared of Christ.[1]

9. For in him dwelleth all the fulness of the Godhead bodily.

> *dwelleth.*—" All the fulness of the divine nature dwells in His body," says Pelagius; that is, truly or corporeally, *i.e.*, the fulness of the Godhead dwelt in His body.

---

8. [1] This gloss is an abbreviation of the following note from Primasius:—
" Contra philosophos agit quorum omnis disputatio de elementis est et visibilibus creaturis et qui ex rebus naturalibus virtutem œstimant Dei, dicentes ex nihilo fieri nihil posse, et animam aut initium non habere, aut esse mortalem, et virginem parere non posse, et Deum ex homine nasci mori atque resurgere stultum esse credere."

11. Putting off the body of the sins of the flesh by the circumcision of Christ.

> *circumcision.*—Question: What is the circumcision of Christ? The answer is not difficult: it means His death and burial: it is these that effect a circumcision from vices.

12. Buried with him in baptism.

> *baptism.*—Three waves pass over us in baptism, because He was three days in the sepulchre.[1]

14. Blotting out the handwriting of ordinances[2] that was against us, which was contrary to us, and took it out of the way, nailing it to his cross.

> *ordinances* (or, *decree*).—Death was decreed to us.
> *nailing it.*—So that it was drowned in His blood.

18. Let no man beguile you of your reward in a voluntary humility and worshipping of angels.

> *beguile you.*—Though they say visions appear to them, and that angels visit them, do not believe it.[3]

20. Wherefore, if ye be dead with Christ from the rudiments of the world, why, as though living in the world, are ye subject to ordinances?

> *rudiments.*—If you have forsaken the desires of the flesh through the death of Christ, why do you again make friends with them? The rudiments of the world, Pelagius says, are avarice, luxury, and the like.

---

12. [1] This was the reason generally assigned for this custom by the Greek writers. Another, which Augustine gives, is, that "it was a symbol of the Trinity." See Eph. iv. 5. Trine immersion was ordered in the First Prayer Book of Edward VI. The Rubric is: "Then the Priest shall take the child in his hands, and ask the name: and naming the child, shall dip it in the water thrice," &c. The word "thrice" was omitted in the Second Prayer Book, and in all editions thereafter.

14. [2] Decree.—Rh. V.

18. [3] Nemo ficta humilitate superbus et angelos se videre mentiens frustra se super homines jactet qui visiones a suo corde loquitur: [sive nemo tam humilis sibi et religiosus videatur ut angelos qui Deum vident se videre mentiatur.]—Pelagius. The former part of this note only was taken by Primasius.

CHAP. III.

> 5. Mortify therefore your members which are upon the earth: fornication, uncleanness, inordinate affection, evil concupiscence, and covetousness, which is idolatry.
>
>> *members.*—These are the members of the old man, and the old man himself is the sum of vices. Each of them is a member, and collectively they form the body.[1]
>
> 16. Let the word of Christ dwell in you richly in all wisdom.
>
>> *dwell.*—Let it dwell, and not merely be with you for a while: the dwelling means preaching and practising it.
>
> 22. Servants, obey in all things your masters according to the flesh.
>
>> *obey.*—Here he commands servants to obey and serve their masters, that the masters may not say, Our servants were obedient unto us before the faith came, but they became disobedient afterwards. He does not like this language, he says, for it was not to teach disobedience he came.

CHAP. IV.

> 2. Continue in prayer, and watch in the same with thanksgiving.
>
>> *continue.*—This is the service due to the heavenly Lord, and he addresses this [advice] to all. The prayer of the slothful and sleepy is powerless, says Pelagius, to obtain anything.
>
> 3. Praying also for us, that God would open unto us a door of utterance to speak the mystery of Christ.
>
>> *mystery of Christ.*—That is, the Gospel, *i.e.*, that we may make manifest the mystery of the incarnation and birth of Christ, and of His passion.

---

5. [1] See Romans vi. 3.

1 TIMOTHY.

CHAP. I.

7. Desiring to be teachers of the law.

teachers.—That they might be engaged in framing laws with kings.[1]

9. The law is not made for a righteous man, but for . . . . manslayers.

manslayers.—Those who slay their kindred.[2]

19. Holding faith, and a good conscience; which some having put away, concerning faith have made shipwreck.

put away.—They separated from it. Their names are mentioned, that no one might follow their example. The Alexander mentioned was an artizan, as he says, "Alexander the coppersmith did me much evil." (2 Tim. iv. 14.)

20. Whom I have delivered unto Satan, that they may learn not to blaspheme.

to Satan.—To repentance: or, to madness.[3]

---

7. [1] This appears to be an allusion to the story of the revision of the laws of Ireland in St. Patrick's time: "The Seanchus and Feinechus of Ireland were purified and written, the writings and old books of Ireland having been collected and brought to one place at the request of St. Patrick. These were the nine supporting props by whom this was done: Laeghaire, King of Ireland, Corc, and Daire, the three kings; Patrick, Benen, and Cairnech, the three saints; Ross, Dubhthach, and Fearghus, the three antiquaries."—*Annals of the Four Masters*, A.D. 438.

9. [2] That is, one of the tribe, each tribe forming an independent kingdom, and legislating for itself. This limits the sixth commandment, according to Irish usage.

20. [3] See 1 Cor. v. 5.

CHAP. II.

4. Who will have all men to be saved, and come unto the knowledge of the truth.

> *all men to be saved.*—Question : Why are not all men saved if He desires it, for the Psalmist says, "He hath done whatsoever he hath pleased" (Ps. cxv. 3)? The answer is not difficult : because no one is constrained against his will : or, a part is put for the whole, for there is no race or language in the world, of which some one was not saved : or, it was those only whom He desired to save that He did save ; *i.e.*, "who will have all men to be saved," that is, Augustine says, as much as to say, no one can be saved except him whom He wills.[1]

5. For there is one God, and one mediator between God and men, the man Christ Jesus.

> *one God.*—As He is the one God of all, He desires the salvation of all.
> *mediator.*—Between Himself and man.

11. Let the woman learn in silence with all subjection.

> *in silence.*—Let them not enquire about anything in church, but "ask their husbands at home." (1 Cor. xiv. 35.)

12. I suffer not a woman to teach.

> *teach.*—Except her own children.

---

4. [1] There are three interpretations proposed in this gloss. The enquiry in the first is Primasius' : "Quare non omnes salventur?" But the answer appears that of Pelagius, viz., the freedom of the will. "Hinc probatus nemini oportere ad credendum vim inferre nec tollere arbitrii libertatem. Sed et illud hoc loco solvitur de indu ratione Pharaonis et cæteræ hujusmodi objectiones et questiones."

The second explanation is that of Primasius : "Juxta figuram synechdochen hic omnes a parte totum debemus accipere." The third is Augustine's.

CHAP. III.

1. If a man desire the office of a bishop, he desireth a good work.

    good work.—Precedence in martyrdom: or, doing the works of a bishop.

2. A bishop must be blameless, the husband of one wife.

    husband.—Before receiving orders, and after baptism.

3. Not given to wine.

    wine.—He does not drink until he is intoxicated.

11. Even so must their wives[1] be grave, not slanderous, sober.

    wives (or, *women*).—For there were deaconesses there at that time.[2]

12. Let the deacons be the husbands of one wife.

    husbands.—Before receiving orders.[3]

13. For they that have used the office of a deacon well[2] purchase to themselves a good degree.

    degree.—Reward in the heavenly kingdom: or, it is right to confer the rank of bishop on them.[4]

---

11. [1] Women.—R.V. and Rh. V.

3. [2] The order of deaconess was discouraged in the west in the sixth century, and soon died out, but continued in the east until the eleventh. "Unde intelligitur" (says Pelagius) "quod de his dicat quas adhuc hodie in Oriente diaconissas appellant."

12. [3] This does not mean, Primasius says, that they *must* be married, but that they must not have two wives. "Non ut, si non habuerint, ducant: sed ne duas habuerint." Marriage in the Greek Church must still take place before ordination.

13. [4] There is a story of St. Columba, when a deacon, having gone to Bishop Etchen to receive consecration as a bishop, but by mistake the order conferred on him was that of presbyter.

"It was not always necessarily required that a man should be ordained presbyter first in order to be made a bishop, for deacons were as commonly made bishops as any other."—*Bingham's Antiq.*, Book II., Chap. x., § 5.

16. And without controversy great is the mystery of godliness: God was manifest in the flesh.

> *manifest.*—The angels knew it; for He reigned over them: or, it was manifested to us by angels on the night of His Nativity.[1]

CHAP. IV.

1. The Spirit speaketh expressly, that in the latter times some shall depart from the faith, giving heed to seducing spirits.

> *depart.*—Though it is most certain that this happened, there will be a time when it will be disbelieved and denied.

7. Refuse profane and old wives' fables, and exercise thyself rather unto godliness.

> *fables.*—Old tales of the law, which the false apostles relate.

8. Bodily exercise profiteth little.[2]

> *little* (or, *for a little*).—Not for long is the beauty of the body.

CHAP. V.

18. For the Scripture saith, Thou shalt not muzzle the ox that treadeth out the corn.

> *Scripture saith.*—This is an example from the Old Law to confirm the principle that it is right to supply food and clothing to the clergy and students.

19. Against an elder receive not an accusation, but before two or three witnesses.

> *two or three witnesses.*—Unless the two laws, the Old and the New, convict him; or, the three laws, the Old, the New, and the Law of Nature.

CHAP. VI.

9. They that will be rich fall into temptation and a snare.

> *temptation.*—They have a constant craving.

---

16. [1] Primasius assigns two reasons, one of which is the second given here: "Quando multitudo angelorum dicebant, 'Gloria in excelsis.'"

8. [2] For a little.—R.V., margin.

2 TIMOTHY.

CHAP. I.

6. Stir[1] up the gift of God, which is in thee by the putting on of my hands.

  stir up.—Even if it was dormant for a while, through fear of trials.

9. According to his own purpose and grace, which was given us in Christ Jesus before the world began.

  given us.—According to the custom of the prudent man, who buys land for his children even before he has any, so He purposed (or wrought) our salvation even before we existed at all.

13. Hold fast the form of sound[2] words, which thou hast heard of me.

  sound (or, *healthful*).—Which heal both body and soul.

CHAP. II.

16. Shun profane and vain babblings: for they will increase unto more ungodliness.

  babblings.—Philosophy and dialectics.

17. Their word will eat as a canker; of whom is Hymenæus and Philetus.

  canker.—A cancer is a disease which is incurable when the virus reaches the heart; thus, says Pelagius, the talk of heretics is to be avoided.

18. Who concerning the truth have erred, saying that the resurrection is past already.

  past.—They consider the resurrection to mean the sons succeeding the fathers; or, the people of God coming forth from captivity.[3]

22. Flee youthful lusts.

  lusts.—Pride and restlessness.

---

6. [1] Stir into flame.—R.V.
13. [2] Healthful.—R.V.
18. [3] Primasius gives three interpretations here, two of which are the same as the following from Pelagius: " Dicentes resurrectionem [est] in filiis; sive ossa vivificata in Ezechiele Israelis interpretabantur de captivitate collecta quasi resurrexisse."

CHAP. III.

8. Now as Jannes and Jambres withstood Moses, so do these also resist the truth.

Jannes and Jambres.—Two Egyptian Druids who were contending with Moses; but he does not reckon it the law,[1] but a legend he had become acquainted with, for he was skilled in all antiquity.

16. All Scripture is given by inspiration of God, and is profitable for doctrine.

inspiration.—Which was inspired to Patriarchs, Prophets, and Apostles.

CHAP IV.

2. Preach the word; be instant in season, out of season.

preach.—Whether any one likes it or dislikes it, preach to him.

14. Alexander the coppersmith did me much evil: the Lord reward him according to his works.

coppersmith.—A tradesman who made idols of brass.

reward.—He wishes evil to evil-doers: or, it is not a wish, but a prophecy;[2] it is not meet that he come with thee; avoid him.

TITUS.

CHAP. I.

3. Hath in due times manifested his word through preaching, which is committed unto me.

manifested.—The life which He promised, that is, the Word, He manifested when it seemed to Him seasonable. It was entrusted to me according to His will, as in the words: "Separate me Barnabas and Saul for the work whereunto I have called them" (Acts xiii. 2); or, "Go ye, therefore, and teach all nations" (Matt. xxviii. 19).

---

8. [1] He calls the history of Moses the law.—Swete's Theodore of Mopsuestia, I., p. 117.
14. [2] The Lord will render to him.—R.V.

5. For this cause left I thee in Crete, that thou shouldest set in order the things that are wanting.

left thee.—Arranging the conferring of orders.
wanting.—To our faith.

12. One of themselves, even a prophet of their own, said, The Cretians are alway liars, evil beasts, slow bellies.

liars.—Thou seest the witness that their own poet gave, that one ought to beware of them, and to instruct them. The prophet referred to was either Epimenides or Callimachus.
evil beasts.[1]—Evil beasts who pour forth blood from cruelty.
slow bellies.—greedy; continually begging for dinners.

15. Unto the pure all things are pure.

all.—All our members: mind, body, soul, thoughts, acts.

CHAP. II.

2. That the aged men be sober, grave, temperate.

sober.—Delightful is a sober old man.

4. Teach the young women to be sober, to love their husbands, to love their children.

love their children.—By correcting them.

CHAP. III.

4. But after that the kindness and love of God our Saviour toward man appeared.

love.—It was of His great love Christ took on Him our human nature.

PHILEMON.

15. Perhaps he therefore departed for a season, that thou shouldest receive him for ever.

for ever.—To be thy servant for ever: or, to be for ever in the faith.

---

12. [1] Fierce men.—Gloss.

HEBREWS.

CHAP. I.

3. When he had by himself purged our sins.

purged.—Through the passion of His body [which was effectual], as He was the brightness of His Father's glory, and the express image of His person.

4. Being made so much better than the angels, as he hath by inheritance obtained a more excellent name than they.

angels.—The angels who administered the Old Law.

5. Thou art my Son, this day have I begotten thee.

son.—A true son by nature, not by adoption.
day.—The day of the manifestation of the Godhead.

7. Who maketh his angels spirits, and his ministers a flame of fire.

spirits.—To breathe, or inspire, salvation to every one.
flame.—To take vengeance on sinners.

11. They shall perish, but thou remainest; and they all shall wax old as doth a garment.

perish.—Their form and appearance only, not their substance.

13. To which of the angels said he at any time, Sit on my right hand, until I make thine enemies thy footstool?

sit.—The Godhead it was that thus addressed the humanity. Then [only] will His enemies be under His feet, when the prison of hell shall be closed on devils and sinners.
footstool.—Under the power of the humanity.

CHAP. II.

1. Therefore we ought to give the more earnest heed to the things which we have heard, lest at any time we should let them slip.[1]

slip (or, *drift away*).—That we may not lapse into perdition, after the manner of a swift stream.

---

1. [1] Drift away from them.—R.V.

8. But now we see not yet all things put under him.
   under him.—While sinners and devils are committing sin.

9. That he, by the grace of God, should taste death for every man.
   taste.—It was a draught [only] of the cup, not lasting death.

10. To make the captain of their salvation perfect through sufferings.
    make perfect.—That He should be exalted from the humiliation of the flesh.

16. He took not on him the nature of angels, but he took on him the seed of Abraham.
    seed.—From them He received the flesh, and He redeemed them, that He might save those who have the same nature.

18. For in that he himself hath suffered, being tempted, he is able to succour them that are tempted.
    succour.—As He saved Himself [in His temptation], He will save all those who believe in Him.

CHAP. III.

1. Wherefore, holy brethren, partakers of the heavenly calling, consider the Apostle and High Priest of our profession,[1] Christ Jesus.
   profession (or, *confession*).—Whom we confess. Moses also was an apostle, because he was sent from God; but they are not alike.

12. Take heed, brethren, lest there be in any of you an evil heart of unbelief in departing from the living God.
    take heed.—Take heed, O people of the New Testament, for the children of Israel at first received some favour.
    departing.—[And returning to] the Old Law.

---

1. [1] Confession.—R.V. and Rh. V.

16. For some, when they had heard, did provoke: howbeit not all that came out of Egypt by Moses.
  not all.—Joshua and Caleb excepted.

17. With whom was he grieved forty years? was it not with them that had sinned, whose carcases fell in the wilderness?
  wilderness.—That was their burial-ground.[1]

18. To whom sware he that they should not enter into his rest?
  rest.—In the land of promise: or, rest in mind through the faith of the Gospel.

CHAP. IV.

2. For unto us was the gospel preached,[2] as well as unto them.
  the gospel (or, *it*).—That is, the land of promise.

4. And God did rest the seventh day from all his works.
  rest.—There was a rest for God after the creation of the world; a rest for the people of Israel in the land of promise; a rest for the people of God in the kingdom of heaven.

12. For the word of God is quick and powerful, and sharper than any two-edged sword, piercing even to the dividing[3] asunder of soul and spirit, and of the joints and marrow, and is a discerner of the thoughts and intents of the heart.
  two-edged sword.—The union of His divine and human nature: or, the incarnation, calling, passion, &c., from the beginning of the "accepted time."
  dividing asunder (or, *unto the division*).—As far as there is a division between them.

---

17. [1] Nothing is more painful to the Irish people than the thought of being buried in an unknown grave, away from their kindred.
2. [2] It hath been declared.—Rh. V.
12. [3] Unto the division.—Rh. V.

The soul and the spirit are one part [of man], and the flesh is another, but the division of them is understood by the Word of God: or, it is the division of soul and spirit: the soul itself is the animal life; the spirit is the spiritual reason in the soul: but how the soul and the grace of God are distributed (or distinguished) the Word of God knows.

CHAP. V.

7. And was heard in that he feared.[1]

feared (or, *for His reverence*).—Because He was the Son of God.

13. For every one that useth milk is unskilful in the word of righteousness; for he is a babe.

milk.—Pottage; solid food is unsuited to you.

CHAP. VI.

19. Which hope we have as an anchor of the soul.

anchor.—When the ship's anchor is let down, the ship cannot be moved; so also is it with the mind when intent [on an object]. Every ship's anchor is cast downwards, but we [Christians] cast our anchor upwards.

---

7. [1] For His reverence.—Rh. V.; *i.e.*, on account of the reverence due to Him.

APPENDIX.

REMARKS ON SOME OF THE SOURCES OF EARLY IRISH THEOLOGY.

THE Würtzburg text of St. Paul's Epistles belongs to what is known as the British type, the basis being the Vulgate, with many Old Latin readings. Most of these are from Ambrosiaster and Sedulius[1] Scotus, junr.; a few from Cyprian and others. It has the peculiarity of placing the Epistle to the Colossians after 2 Thessalonians. This is the order in two other manuscripts of the Irish school, the Codex Boernerianus of St. Gall, and the Book of Armagh; it is also found in Augustine[2], Primasius, and Isidore,[3] of Seville, all of whom are quoted in these glosses. Although the Irish glosses cease at Hebrews vii. 5, the text continues to chap. xii. 24. Unlike the glosses, it is in the handwriting of one scribe throughout, and exhibits that peculiar spelling which characterizes all Latin manuscripts of the Middle Ages which are the work of Irish scribes. Professor Zimmer attributes this to the influence of their native language.

PELAGIUS is the chief authority in the glosses. He is quoted forty-two times by name in the Latin passages, and is also the source of many of the Irish, though not named in them. He was a very popular writer, notwithstanding his opinions. "This great heresiarch" (to quote Bishop Lightfoot) "wrote his Commentary on the thirteen Epistles of St. Paul at Rome. In the middle of the sixth century, when Cassiodorus wrote, learned men assigned them

---

[1] There are six of these:—Rom. ii. 27; iii. 9; vii. 18; 1 Cor. xii. 13; 2 Cor. i. 11; Gal. iv. 2.
[2] Westcott, *Canon of the New Testament*, 3rd edition, p. 528.
[3] *Ibid.*, p. 537.

to Pope Gelasius. At a later date they were fathered on St. Jerome, and are generally printed in the editions of his works. Cassiodorus, finding the Commentary tainted with Pelagian errors, expurgated the Epistle to the Romans by removing the heretical passages, and thus set an example, as he tells us, which might be followed more easily by others on the remaining Epistles. In its present form, then, this Commentary is mutilated. The notes are pointed and good, but meagre. The high estimation in which they were held, in spite of the cloud which hung over their author, and the fact of their being attributed both to Gelasius and to Jerome, are high testimonies to their merits."[1]

Of the passages quoted in the glosses from Pelagius, twelve[2] are wanting in Migne's edition. Some of these from the Romans, particularly that on v. 15, which contains a reference to his heretical teaching, may be those removed by Cassiodorus. In quoting so extensively from Pelagius, it was unavoidable that his terminology should more or less affect the language of the glosses. An instance of this is the expression "penal death" (*báas péne*). This is a translation of his phrase "*mors æternæ pœna*,"[3] into Irish, with the omission of the word *æternæ*. He held that the death of the body was natural, and that Adam would have died if he had never sinned; from this it followed that the penalty of his transgression must have been the death of the soul, which, therefore, he called "the penal death." In the glosses the phrase is used apparently without any doctrinal reference, as simply equivalent to future punishment. Sometimes passages occur as to which there may be some doubt whether they teach error or not. One is, "It is not more trying for you than for Christ."[4] Mr. Stokes translates this: "Not *more difficult for you;*" and this is the usual sense of the word *annsu*. But as it would imply the mere humanity of Christ, contrary to such glosses as Rom. ix. 5, xv. 8, 12, and to the tenor of the Commentary, and as the word may also mean "more trying or painful,"[5] I

---

[1] Lightfoot on the Galatians, 6th edition, p. 233.
[2] On Romans ii. 23; iv. 17; v. 15; vii. 7; xi. 25; xv. 3; I Cor. ii. 7; iii. 22; v. 13, 19; vii. 35; xi. 28.
[3] On Romans viii. 13.
[4] Romans xv. 3.
[5] *Gravius*. Zeuss. Gram. Celt., 2nd edition, p. 276. Compare also, *is ansu cech todærnam an guin cosind loscud; i.e., An guin cosindsáigit din.* More painful than every agony is a wound with burning, *i.e.*, the wound of a fiery arrow.—P. 917*a*.

have ventured to translate it so. Another passage may be mentioned from a source not yet identified: "The manhood which He received from us makes supplication to the Deity that we may not die."[1] This is probably only inaccurate language.

Pelagius' opinions were refuted by Augustine and Jerome, the anti-Pelagian writings of the former being very numerous. Jerome denounced him in his usual unmeasured language; he says he is "a huge and corpulent Alpine dog, who can do more mischief with his claws than with his teeth, for he is by descent of the Scotic[2] [Irish] nation, the next country to the British; and like another Cerberus, according to the fables of the poets, must be struck down with a spiritual club, that he may be silenced for ever with his master Pluto."[3]

Archbishop Ussher[4] understood Celestius, the follower of Pelagius, to be the person intended here; but Dr. Todd thinks the context requires that it should be referred to Pelagius, who is otherwise known to have been a man of great stature—a Goliath, as he is termed by another author. This view seems to be supported by the term "Alpinum," *i.e.*, of Alba,[5] or Scotland. There seems to have been an occasional passage of colonists to Scotland from the north of Ireland from the middle of the third century[6] onward, until 506, when the regular settlement of Argyleshire took place. If Pelagius belonged to a family of Irish origin, who were settled in Alba, this would explain why Augustine calls him a Briton, and how at the same time he was descended from the Scotic [Irish] nation, the next country to the British.

After Jerome's language it is pleasant to read Augustine's opinion of him. He says he was "a man of most acute genius;" "a man

---

[1] Romans viii. 34.
[2] Ireland was called Scotia until the eleventh century.
[3] Todd's *St. Patrick*, pp. 190-192. Dr. Todd says he is unable to see the "vis consequentiæ" of the "for;" but it seems to mean that, being of Irish descent, fighting was more congenial to him than arguing.
[4] Works, Vol. V., 254.
[5] Alba, Alpa, and sometimes Elpa, was the ancient name of Scotland. So in the hymn of Fiacc, *Do faid tar Elpa huite*. This the scholiast explains as "he went over the mount of Albion," *i.e.*, Drumalban, the great mountain chain dividing Perthshire and Argyle, and terminating in the Grampian Hills. He adds: "Albion was formerly a name for the whole island of Britain."—*Tripartite Life of St. Patrick*, Roll's Edition, II., 405.
[6] Reeves' *Ecclesiastical Antiquities of Down, Connor, and Dromore*, p. 319.

of holy and most Christian life;" and "one whom he greatly loved." This is high testimony from an antagonist.

Reference is made in the gloss on 1 Cor. iv. 13 to his knowledge of Greek. He was evidently well acquainted with the language, for at the Synod of Jerusalem, where he was accused by Orosius, a Spanish presbyter sent by Augustine for the purpose, we find him addressing the Council in Greek, which his accuser was unable to do.

The Preface to the Epistles in the *Book of Armagh*, as well as the separate Prefaces to each Epistle, are by Pelagius.

ISIDORE OF SEVILLE is quoted but once, and does not appear to have had much influence in Ireland.

GREGORY THE GREAT, however, was held in much esteem. His accession "to the Chair and successorship of Peter the Apostle," is recorded in the "Annals of the Four Masters" (A.D. 590), where he is termed "of the golden mouth." He is called in the *Martyrology of Donegal*, "Gregory of the Morals," from the *Libri moralium* which he composed; an abstract of this work was made by a Saint named Laidchenn (*d.* 661), of whom little more is known. This circumstance shews at what an early period the Irish became acquainted with his writings. How highly they esteemed him[1] may be judged from their conferring on him the compliment of an Irish pedigree. This was effected, Dr. O'Donovan says, by "engrafting him on the royal stem of Conaire the Second," and then deducing his descent in regular form.

AUGUSTINE was known in Ireland, as elsewhere; and his name is found in the *Calendar of Oengus Cele De*, at August 28th, simply as "the conspicuous one from Africa." The Irish were fond of finding parallels for their native saints, and the *Martyrology of Donegal*, at September 3, states that a saint named Longarad was "in his habits and life like unto Augustine, who was very wise." His influence is perceptible in these glosses, especially in the Epistle to the Romans.

JEROME is more frequently quoted by Irish theologians than

---

[1] In one point of view there is a parallel between the glosses and Archbishop Trench's *Notes on the Parables and Miracles*. He seems to have admired Gregory, whom he often quotes; and he also quotes Eastern and Western writers of many schools of thought, even those, such as Maldonatus, to whom he was entirely opposed in doctrine.

Augustine. The *Book of Armagh* contains his Preface to the Four Gospels, and his Prologue to the Galatians. His Preface to the Gospel of St. John is also quoted in the Evangelistarium of St. Molling (690). The *Calendar of Oengus*, at September 30, mentions him as "the sage, sound, eloquent, long-lived Hieronymus of Bethlehem;" and for him also a parallel is found by the *Martyrology of Donegal*, at Jan. 24, in a saint named Manchan, who "in habits and life was like unto Hieronymus, who was very learned." They oddly called him "Cirine," finding this easier to pronounce, as no Irish name begins with H. They treated the initial as equivalent to Ch or to C.

ORIGEN, though only mentioned once, exercised much influence on this work. The allegorical interpretations which so often occur are in accordance with his method, and the glosses on several texts appear to express his peculiar views. The omission, as already mentioned, of "*æternæ*" from Pelagius' phrase for future punishment, when translated in the gloss, may be due to the influence of his belief in the non-eternity of punishment.

To his speculations, also, we may probably ascribe the gloss on "*apocalypsin*" (1 Cor. xiv. 26). The note of Primasius on the passage is simply "revelatio mysteriorum," translated into Irish (*foilsigud rúun*), but to this the Irish commentator prefixes "memoria" as an explanation. It seems difficult to attach any meaning to this, if it does not imply Plato's doctrine of "*anamnesis*," or recollection, which the Irish may have learned either directly from his works, or through the medium of Origen and the neo-Platonists. Plato's account of knowledge was that it was the recalling to mind what had been learnt in a previous state of existence. Thus in the *Meno*, Socrates explains it: "The soul, then, as being immortal, and having been born again many times, and having seen all things that there are, whether in this world or the world below, has knowledge of them all, and it is no wonder she should be able to call to remembrance all that she ever knew about virtue, and about everything; for as all nature is akin, and the soul has learned all things, there is no difficulty in her eliciting, or, as men say, learning, all out of a single recollection, for all enquiry and all learning is but recollection."[1] The belief in the pre-existence of

---

[1] *Dialogues of Plato* (Jowett), Oxford, 1871, Vol. I., p. 269.

souls was held by Origen; and it is, perhaps, allowable to conjecture that this gloss represents a combination of the theory of "*anamnesis*" with Christian teaching, the recovery of the lost knowledge being in this case aided by the spiritual illumination of the Corinthian, to whom mysteries were thus revealed.[1] But independently of Origen the Irish also studied Plato himself, as appears from the twelfth century copy of Chalcidius' translation of the *Timæus*, and his commentary on it, which is in the Bodleian Library. This manuscript has many glosses in the Irish language, which is an evidence that it was used by Irish students. The glosses have been published by Mr. Whitley Stokes,[2] who observes: "The Celts seem to have studied Chalcidius, and there is some reason to think that the knowledge of Plato possessed by Johannes Scotus Erigena was obtained through the medium of Chalcidius' translation and commentary."[3] This famous Irishman was a contemporary of the authors of these glosses.

If a conjecture may be hazarded, the first part of the gloss on Romans xi. 33 suggests a passage[4] in Chalcidius, allowance being made for the difficulty of expressing philosophical ideas in Irish. "The things which belong to the secret meaning which was in the mysteries of the Godhead in creating the elements in the beginning"[5] appear to have some connexion with the *archetypa exemplaria*, the "original models" of which he speaks. It would seem to have been from the same source that Erigena derived his Realism.

HILARY.—Among the commentaries used, but not named, is that formerly attributed to St. Ambrose, and still published with his works, though now known not to be his. When the mistake was

---

[1] It may be said that as recollection supposes an effort of mind, it does not apply in the present instance; but one of Plato's definitions seems to meet the case: ἀνάμνησις δ'ἐστιν ἐπιρροὴ φρονήσεως ἀπολιπούσης.—Meno, 81 D. in *Astius' Lexicon Platonicum*, Lipsiæ, 1835.

[2] Kuhn's Zeitschrift für Vergleichende sprachforschung. Band, xxix. ss. 372-379.

[3] M. Haureau says: "Il parait avoir lu le Timée dans le texte original." (*Histoire de la Philosophie Scolastique*, 2nd Ed., Part I., pp. 148-175.) But he was not aware that the Irish were acquainted with this translation.

[4] He refers in it to "species quas concipientes mente dicimus semper separatas a coetu corporearum specierum fore *archetypa exemplaria* rei sensilis."

[5] Isdo tiagait indrétaisin huili dontlathur diasndísiu robói hirúnaib innadeacte octuiste dúile hitossuch.

discovered, the author came to be known as Ambrosiaster, which, however, is only a negative name, signifying that he is not the real Ambrose. Augustine quotes it as by St. Hilary, *i.e*, the Deacon. Bishop Lightfoot unites the two names, calling him the Ambrosian Hilary. Hilary was a native of Sardinia, and was sent, together with Lucifer of Cagliari, and Pancratius, by Pope Liberius to the Emperor Constantius after the Synod of Arles, with a view to obtain the assembling of a fresh council. When Lucifer and Eusebius of Vercellœ, were banished to the Thebaid by the Emperor (355-361), Hilary is said to have been banished with them. Mr. Haddan, referring to the agreement of the Latin translation of the Scriptures used by Gildas and St. Patrick with some passages found in Lucifer of Cagliari, says, "One is at a loss to see any possibility of association between Britain and Sardinia."[1] There may have been no connexion between the countries; but the connexion of Lucifer with Hilary, who was known, as we find here, to the Irish, seems to establish a link; and if he was also banished to the Thebaid with him, and spent six years there, the known intercourse of Ireland with Egypt[2] makes it highly probable that they had some acquaintance with his writings. There are two readings[3] from Lucifer in the present text.

The Ambrosian Hilary, as he may be termed, with Bishop Lightfoot, is represented in the text by seven readings[4] and some glosses. One of the latter, in Romans ii. 23, is erroneously assigned to Pelagius in the manuscript. The work is considered by Lightfoot as "one of the best Latin Commentaries." A recent writer[5] mentions

---

[1] *Remains of Rev. A. W. Haddan*, p. 217.

[2] For an account of the tour of an Irish party in Egypt, A.D. 825, see Dicuil, *De Mensura Orbis*, cvi., § 3, 1, ed. Letronne, Paris, 1814. Professor Stokes of Dublin praises Dicuil's "extensive learning and accurate geographical research;" (*Ireland and the Celtic Church*, 2nd edition, p. 213); but Mannert formed a different opinion. He has shewn that poor Dicuil, "scriptor miserrimus," as he terms him, mistook a revision of the map of the Empire for a new survey, and thus gave his book its erroneous title. It is highly amusing to hear of the Roman Empire being surveyed in a few months (*mensibus exiguis*), whereas the survey ordered by Julius Cæsar took thirty-two years. See *Tabula Itineraria Peutingeriana*.—C. Mannertus Lipsiæ, 1824.

[3] In Ephesians ii. 3; Hebrews iii. 16.

[4] Romans i. 8; viii. 28; xiv. 10; xvi. 3, 8; Galatians vi. 1.

[5] *Theodori Episcopi Mopsuesteni Commentarii*.—H. B. Swete, D.D., Cambridge, 1880, pp. xiv., xv.

the discovery of a manuscript, the former part of which, as far as Galatians, is the same as this, but the commentary on the remaining Epistles is derived from Theodore of Mopsuestia.

THEODORE of Mopsuestia, known in the East as the Interpreter, was the chief of the school of expositors for which Antioch was famous, whose principle of interpretation was the grammatical and historical, as opposed to the allegorical method of Origen. He is well known in connexion with the controversy of the Three Chapters condemned in the Council of Constantinople (A.D. 553), and as a favourer of the heresy of Nestorius. His Commentary on the Epistles, from Galatians onwards, may have become known to the Irish through the supposed work of St. Ambrose, but there was also another source.

PRIMASIUS, the last to be mentioned as connected with the glosses, flourished in 551. He was Bishop of Adrumetum, in the eastern part of the Province of Africa, the present territory of Tunis. When Pope Vigilius was summoned to Constantinople by the Emperor, and obliged to sign the decrees of the Council,[1] Primasius accompanied him, and while there made the acquaintance of Junilius,[2] a distinguished lawyer. Enquiring who among the Greeks was distinguished as a theologian, Junilius replied, "Paul of Nisibis, a Persian." On further enquiry, he told him he was in possession of an introduction to the Scriptures by him, which, at the solicitation of Primasius, he translated into Latin. Kihn has shown that this work is really founded on the teaching of Theodore of Mopsuestia. Primasius wrote a Commentary on the Epistles of St. Paul and on the Apocalypse, and Kihn[3] discusses the question how far these works are affected by Theodore's teaching, arriving at the conclusion that neither of them shows oriental influence. But since the publication of his work a pamphlet by Dr. Haussleiter[4] has appeared.

---

[1] This is the Pope to whom Columbanus refers in his letter to Boniface the Fourth, in which he says: "Vigila quia forte non bene vigilavit Vigilius," &c. —Lanigan, *Ecc. Hist.*, II., 294.

[2] See Dr. Salmon's article on Junilius in the "Dictionary of Christian Biography."

[3] Theodor von Mopsuestia und Junilius Africanus als exegeten. Von Heinrich Kihn, Freiburg in Breisgau, 1880.

[4] Leben und Werke des Bischofs Primasius von Hadrumetum eine untersuchung —Von Dr. J. Haussleiter. Erlangen, 1887.

He considers this enquiry to be merely a waste of time, and has propounded the theory that, though Primasius wrote the Commentary on the Apocalypse, he was not the author of that on the Epistles. He would regard it as three centuries later, and assign it either to Remigius, of Auxerre, 880, or Remigius, of Lyons, 875. If this opinion is accepted, it will be necessary to correct Zeuss' estimate, and instead of assigning the glosses to the end of the eighth or the beginning of the ninth century, they must be placed at the end of the ninth or the beginning of the tenth. The statements of those writers will, no doubt, be tested, and particularly Dr. Haussleiter's dogmatic assertion.[1] It is singular that when Kihn enumerates the writers used by Primasius, as "Jerome, Ambrose, Augustine, and others," to which Haussleiter adds several more, neither he or Kihn seems to be aware that the Commentary is taken chiefly from Pelagius, whom they do not name. This will be evident to the readers of the present work, in which the notes so often mention them together; but it may be well to quote Mr. Swete: "I found [in Primasius] many comments of a decidedly Theodorean type; but with few exceptions they proved to have been taken almost verbatim from Pelagius."[2] Again: "Future editors of Pelagius will probably derive much assistance from Primasius, and possibly from later compilers, into whose pages Pelagius has flowed through the medium of Primasius." Kihn and Haussleiter further refer to Primasius'[3] supposed ignorance of Greek, and the latter founds an argument against his authorship of the Commentary upon the fact that in Galatians ii. 5 the author follows the reading which agrees with the Greek text instead of that of the African Church.[4] It is, however, by no means certain that he was unacquainted with Greek, for, as Mr. Swete observes, "though Kihn infers from the *Constitutum* that Primasius was ignorant of Greek, the words, 'Græcæ linguæ ... sumus ignari' may fairly be limited to Vigilius himself."[5] The Commentary on the Apocalypse is allowed to be taken chiefly from the Donatist writer, Ticonius; but Dr. Haussleiter does not notice the

---

[1] Primasius hat gar keinen Kommentar zu den Paulischen briefe geschrieben.
[2] P. xlv.
[3] *Ib.*, note.
[4] The African text had "ad horam cessimus;" the other, "neque ad horam cessimus."
[5] P. lv., note.

fact that Ticonius is also quoted in the Commentary on the Epistles, which affords some ground for thinking that the author may be the same. For these reasons the reader will probably be disposed to suspend his judgment, and wait for further information on the subject.

The manner in which Primasius deals with Pelagius is instructive. In using a work which, though composed before the publication of Pelagius' opinions, was still of doubtful orthodoxy, he had to be cautious; and accordingly, when he meets with anything he does not approve of in a passage, he omits it, as at Romans xi. 32; or again, he adds what he thinks is required to render a statement orthodox, as at Romans vi. 3; and like our glosses, as at Romans v. 15, he censures Pelagianism, though using Pelagius as his chief authority; and thus, like other early writers, he steers his Commentary through the surrounding dangers.[1]

As this Appendix deals with some of the sources of Irish theology, a reference to two other writers, though unconnected with the glosses, may not be out of place. In the panegyric on St. Colum Cille, termed the "Amra," attributed to Dallan Forgail (590), reference is made to Basil. This was Basil the Great, 370. The Amra is not only Irish of very early date, but it is also intentionally obscure, and has never been fully translated.[2] In it there is a statement with regard to the arrival of St. Colum Cille at the Synod of Drumceatt.[3] The scholiast on this passage, himself an ancient writer, offers two interpretations of it:—1. When received at the Synod, with the performance of an elaborate piece of music (*aidbse*), and the acclamations of the assembly, he was so elated that Baithin found it necessary to quote a passage from St. Basil to abate his pride. Baithin was his successor at Hy (Iona), and accounted "the most learned man on this side the Alps," after Colum Cille. 2. The other interpretation is that the saint studied the works of St. Basil for his own instruction. Whichever view is taken, the fact remains that, when the Amra was written, the works of St. Basil, or some of them at least, were known in Ireland. One of the most popular

---

[1] Primasius' work is one of those which, as Dr. Haussleiter says:—"Die Kirkliche Lehre zwischen der Scylla der Pelagianischen und der Charybdis der Manichäischen Häresis unversehrt durchzuführen versuchten."

[2] A clever attempt was made by O'Beirne Crowe, but it does not stand the test of criticism.

[3] *Armbert bassil brathu.* (Goidelica), 2nd Ed., p. 163.

of them was the Philocalia, or "beauties of Origen," compiled by him and Gregory of Nazianzus. It had a large circulation, and may possibly have been the work referred to here. In connection with this incident, it is worthy of this notice, that it is said the saint was in danger of being made a god of, or feeling like a god,[1] from the applause of the assembly, which is the language applied to the Apostles in the gloss on 1 Corinthians i. 10: "The disciples treated them as gods."

CASSIAN, the author of the Collations, appears from another passage[2] in the Amra to have been also known to St. Colum Cille. Here the scholiast again offers two interpretations: 1. He read the books of the law, as he read those of John Cassian: or, he read, like Cassian, the books of the law. This does not clearly prove that the saint was acquainted with Cassian, as the meaning is uncertain; but it is an evidence that his works were known when the Amra was written. There is, however, another passage, though of later date, which preserves the tradition about St. Colum Cille. It is one of the Irish glosses on the Latin hymns in the *Liber Hymnorum*, which are assigned to the twelfth century. "Ten [canonical] hours Colum Cille used to celebrate, as it is said, and he took that practice from the history of John Cassian."[3]

If this series of authors is compared with the list of books given to the library of Bobbio by Dungal in the ninth century,[4] or with that of the works in the library of Lerins, mentioned by Greith,[5] it will appear that while several are common to all three, the glosses are singular in taking as their chief authority Pelagius, whose name does not occur in the Continental lists. The writers of the glosses were men of piety; they did not agree with him in his peculiar doctrines; yet they accept him as their teacher, though no heretic of early times was more frequently condemned by Councils.[6]

This seems strange, but it is in accordance with the general attitude of the Irish divines with respect to authority. Thus when Col-

---

[1] *Do bith innadia.*
[2] *Sluinnsius leig libru libuir ut car Cassian* (Goidelica), p. 164.
[3] *Goidelica*, p. 70.
[4] Muratori, *Antiq. Ital.* Dissert. 43, Tom. III., N. 821.
[5] *Altirische Kirche*, p. 68.
[6] At Brevi, Carthage, Milevi, Rome, Byzacum, Orange, and the Third General Council (Ephesus).

man,[1] Bishop of Lindisfarne, in the Conference at Whitby, was pressed with the argument that the Council of Nice was against him, he took no notice of it: it carried no weight with him; he would follow the customs of his Church regardless of its decisions. And Columbanus, when the same arguments were addressed to him, reinforced by French Synods, did not yield: and when continued pressure was brought to bear on him, he appealed to the Council of Constantinople,[2] which recognised the liberties of "the Churches among the barbarous nations." It may be said that in this he admitted the authority of a Council, but the appeal was rather an *argumentum ad hominem*, and a claim to freedom from authority, founded on the admission contained in the Canon referred to. Later again, when Boniface, Archbishop of Mentz, complained to the Pope of the Irish clergy in his diocese, he says of Clement,[3] amongst other things, that he "rejects the Canons of the Churches, and despises the authority of Synods." We have evidently here a uniform line of action: the Irish would not submit to mere authority. Alcuin (A.D. 780), who was the contemporary of several eminent Irishmen, states their position thus: "Authority and custom had little weight with them, unless some reason was added to authority."[4] On the other hand, it was considered sufficient by the clergy on the Continent to produce a *catena* of venerable names in support of any proposition. One reason of the attitude of the Irish was that those were foreign Councils to them. This is implied in the claim of Columbanus, that his Church was one of those "among the barbarous nations," and therefore free. The term "barbarous" is uniformly applied to the Irish in the middle ages, not as a name of reproach, but as simply meaning "foreign," which is the interpretation given in the gloss on Romans i. 14. Those Councils called by Roman Emperors, and held on Roman soil, were in their eyes Councils of the Empire, to which they as foreigners owed no allegiance. What they claimed, then, was intellectual freedom, not from a desire to depart from the faith, but because they felt it to be

---

[1] Bede's *Eccl. Hist.*, Lib. III., Cap. XXV.
[2] Lanigan's *Eccl. Hist.*, II., 272.
[3] Ussher's Works, IV., 457.
[4] Quoted in Mullinger's *Schools of Charles the Great*, p. 119.

their right. And it is at this period only that the true bent of the native intellect can be discerned, for in after times the inroads of the Danes led to vital changes in the religious life of the people. In their crusade against Christianity they massacred the clergy, or drove them to seek shelter in foreign lands, and did their utmost to destroy the literature of the Church. A native writer thus describes their procedure: "The writings and the books in every church and in every sanctuary where they were, were burned and thrown into the water by the plunderers from the beginning to the end;"[1] that is, from the beginning to the end of the Danish sway in Ireland, this was their uniform course. This literature must have been very large, for, as Dr. Atkinson[2] has observed, "At a very early period the country was full of scribes;" but of all the manuscripts then existing four only survive in Ireland, and about two hundred on the Continent, which escaped destruction by being carried away:[3] one of these is the manuscript now at Würtzburg, which contains these glosses. Thus it came to pass that when King Brian, on the decline of the Danish power at the end of the tenth century, wished to revive religion, "he was obliged to send professors and masters" (the same native authority tells us) "to buy books beyond the sea and the great ocean; and Brian himself gave the price of learning and the price of books to every one separately who went on this service."[4] Here we have clearly defined the period when the old order gave place to the new. The phase of religion then existing on the Continent was reproduced here, and the change is seen in the Book of Leinster, belonging to the middle of the 12th century, the Lebor Brecc, and other compilations, which contain much that is wholly different in character from these glosses. By this action of Brian the way was prepared for the famous Malachy, Archbishop of Armagh, whose great merit, according to St. Bernard,[3] was, that "he established in all the Churches the Apostolic constitutions and the decrees of the holy fathers, but especially the customs of the holy Church of Rome."[5]

---

[1] *Wars of the Gaedhil with the Gaill*, Rev. J. H. Todd, D.D., p. 139 (Roll's Ed.).
[2] Todd Lecture Series, Vol. II., p. 36. Dublin: 1887.
[3] Zimmer, *Keltische Studien*, ss. 25-27.
[4] *Wars of the Gaedhil*, as above.
[5] *Vita Mal.*, Cap. III.

A few observations on Irish monasticism are suggested by a reference to Cassian, which occurs in the Calendar of Œngus. Cassian introduced the monastic system from Egypt into southern Gaul: from Gaul it reached Ireland. The origin of that system is generally ascribed to Anthony, who gathered those persons who had been leading a solitary life in the deserts of Egypt into communities, and framed rules for them. Mr. Fergusson, however, having called attention to the close intercourse, commercial and other, which existed between Egypt and India in very early times, points out that similar associations had been in existence among the Indian Buddhists for more than three hundred years before Anthony's time,[1] and he suggests that he obtained the idea from them. This seems to derive some confirmation from two legends of Irish saints, one of whom is directly connected with Cassian, and thus with Egypt. In the Calendar of Œngus, at November 25th, is the entry: "Findchu of Brigobann went with John Cassian, whose crown is very fair, into Croch, a fair country."[2] This saint flourished probably in the sixth century, and is still locally remembered at Brigown, or Mitchelstown. The Calendar tells us he had a "prison," or cell, roofed with flags, in which two iron hooks were inserted: on these he suspended himself by his armpits, "so that his head did not strike against the stone above, nor his feet against the floor."[3] According to a later form of the legend, he remained seven years in this position. The idea of such a way of mortifying the flesh can hardly be of native origin. It looks like an imitation of the practice of the Indian devotee who gets himself suspended by a hook fixed in his flesh. Another legend is that of St. Ite, of Killeedy, in the County of Limerick, whose name "Thirst" is in allusion to Psalm xlii. 2. She had a stag-beetle which she applied to her side, and allowed to gnaw her flesh. "Bigger than a lapdog was it" (says Œngus), "and it destroyed the whole of one of her sides. No one knew of this secret self-torture. Once, when she went out of her cell, the beetle followed her; the nuns saw it, and killed it. Ite enquired why the beetle came not to her;

---

[1] *Rude Stone Monuments*, p. 503.
[2] *The Calendar of Œngus*. By Whitley Stokes, LL.D. (Royal Irish Academy), p. clxxii. The name Brigobann (Brigown), or "Smiths' hill," is said to have been given in commemoration of the skill of the smiths who manufactured the hooks.
[3] *The Martyrology of Donegal*, p. 317.

'why has my fosterling gone?' she said. 'Do not rob us of heaven,' say the nuns; 'it is we that killed him.'"[1] This might seem the invention of a distempered imagination; but, stripped of its exaggeration, as to the size of the beetle, &c., "it reminds one" (Mr. Whitley Stokes observes) "of a mode of torture sometimes practised in India. Half a cocoa-nut shell, with a large stag-beetle inside, is fastened to the victim's body. The beetle struggles to escape, and at last endeavours to burrow through the flesh."[2] Findchu also appears to have practised this self-torture, for in his Life, in the Book of Lismore, it is said: "He was ashamed that his perforated body, pierced and holed by chafers and beasts, should be seen." Whether any Irishmen visited India is not known, but it is not improbable. They were famous for their wanderings, and Walafrid Strabo, writing in A.D. 849, says travelling had become a second nature to them. We hear of them visiting Constantinople: they roamed over the Black Sea, and one of the St. Colmans acquired the name of "the Cimmerian wanderer." Passing on eastward, the earliest mention in European literature of the phenomenon known as "the eternal fires," at Baku, on the Caspian, is found in a tenth century Irish Geography.[3] This knowledge could only have been acquired from the personal visit of some Irish pilgrim to the petroleum springs of that remarkable region. In the same Geography is a description of India and its products.

It is therefore within the limits of possibility that some Irishmen, visiting the early home of monasticism, may have brought away a knowledge of the practices of the Indian ascetics, and made them known in their native land.

---

[1] *Œngus*, p. xxxiv.

[2] *Ibid., Glossarial Index*, p. cclxxix.

[3] *The Geography of Ros Ailithir*. By Rev. T. Olden. *Proceedings of the Royal Irish Academy*, 2nd Series, Vol. II., pp. 219-252. This place is now Ross Carbery (Co. Cork).

INDEX.

Abraham, 9, 10, 11.
Abstinence, 39, 40.
Adam, 12, 53, 69, 70, 76, 79, 88, 91.
Adoption, 112.
Advent, 45, 92.
Angel, 23.
Angels, 54, 103, 108.
Apostles, 67, 81, 83.
—— ambassadors, 67, 76.
—— chiefest, 80, 84.
—— treated as gods, 46, 49, 80.
—— false, 49, 79, 80, 83, 85, 108.

Baptism, 13, 35, 46, 47, 51, 64, 107.
—— trine immersion in, 90, 103.
—— confession of faith in, 19.
—— effects of, 19, 62, 72.
Bishops, 107.
Blood of Christ, 8, 92, 103.
—— spiritual, 87.
Body of sin, 13.

Celibacy, 55, 56, 57.
Circumcision, 9.
—— mystical, 9, 56.
Christ prophesied, 2, 6, 82, 90, 104.
—— incarnation of, 2, 6, 27, 44, 45, 90, 111.
—— divine nature of, 24, 41, 74, 90, 93, 94, 99, 102, 112.
—— human nature of, 41, 81, 94, 112.
—— alone without sin, 7.
—— suffered, 20, 22, 39, 40, 91.
—— death of, 14, 39, 71, 103.
—— resurrection of, 13, 14, 15, 21.

Christ, ascension of, 76, 90.
—— body of, 13, 14, 45, 94.
—— do., mystical, 35, 45, 55, 62, 88, 92, 102.
—— do. in Holy Communion, 61.
Church, the whole, 44.
—— in house, 43.

Day of judgment, 98.
Deaconesses, 107.
Death (bodily and penal), 13, 19, 67.
Devil, 14, 99, 100.
Devils, 54, 67.
Druids, 24, 26, 30, 87.

Election, 24, 26, 30, 87.

Faith, 1, 8, 10, 11, 12, 15, 17, 19, 27, 28, 29, 34, 35, 38, 47, 84.
Fall, 31.
Fasting, 39, 80.
Feast of the Lamb, 52.

Glory, 20, 21, 25, 36, 45.
Gospel, 28, 32, 43, 66, 74, 101, 104.
God, eternity of, 3.
—— will of, 34.
Grace, 9, 10, 12, 13, 15, 17, 30, 35, 45, 65, 72.
—— given to all, 35, 89.

Heaven, ranks of, 87.
Heretics, 12, 95.
Holy Spirit, 1, 2, 18, 19, 20, 23, 35, 48, 52, 54, 60, 61, 65, 66, 75, 81, 87, 89, 97.

Idolatry, 30.
Israel, 11, 23, 29, 86.

Jews, 3.
Judgment, 5, 12, 24, 53.
Justification, 5, 9, 12, 18, 24, 53.

Law, 6, 9, 10, 12, 16, 17.
—— preaches, 6.
—— spiritual, 17.
Life, 16.
—— eternal, 13, 19.

Madness, 52, 105.
Martyrdom, 22, 42.
Marriage, 56.
—— of clergy, 107.
Mediation, 22.
Member of Christ, 14, 23, 32, 55, 57, 62.
Merit, 8, 24, 26, 31, 33.
Moses, 17.
Mystery, 6, 28, 33.
—— of God, 64, 75.
—— of the Cross, 47, 63.
—— of the law, 73, 74, 77.

Nature, sinful, 88.

Offering of Christ, 76, 84, 92, 112.

Peace, 12, 28.
Pedagogues, 51.
Philosophy, 48, 102, 109.
Prayer, 20, 34, 36, 63, 96, 104.
Preaching—
—— the Gospel, 2, 32, 83.
—— through Christ, 5, 28, 42, 44, 46, 51, 53, 58, 59, 61, 64, 73, 92, 100.
Prophesying, 35, 60, 64, 66.
Prophets, 28, 29.

Prophets, false, 35, 63, 65.
Punishment, everlasting, 86.

Redemption, 8, 22.
Resurrection, 14.
—— order of, 20, 67, 68, 96.
—— body of Christ, 13, 14.
Repentance, 32, 52, 72.
Reprobate, 81.
Reward, 37, 50, 57.
Righteousness, 11, 26, 27, 28, 30, 93.
—— of Christ, 12.
Rock, 59.

Saints, 8, 21, 25, 62, 92.
Salvation, 11, 25, 27, 33, 44, 76.
Satan, 52, 79, 95.
Sin, 17, 19, 34, 70, 91.
—— not imputed, 12.
—— body of, 13.
—— offering, 76.
—— of Adam, 12, 16.
Sinners, all, 7, 11, 12, 70, 76.
Soul, 17, 34, 64, 69.
Spirit of man, 49.
Spiritual man, 49, 74, 86.

Teaching, 63.
Testaments, 27.
Temple, 89, 99.
Thorn in flesh, 80.
Translation, 61, 65.
Trinity, 54, 100.

Unbelief, 33.

Will, 16, 30, 68.
—— of God, 34.
Wisdom, 34, 36, 47.
—— true, 48.
Women preaching, 60, 66.

AUTHORS QUOTED IN THE GLOSSES.

Augustine, 106.
Gregory, 61.
Isidore, 80.
Jerome, 59, 82.

Origen, 37.
Pelagius, 3, 4, 6, 11, 15, 16, 21, 22, 29, 32, 33, 37, 40, 43, 46, 48, 50, 51, 53, 61, 66.

ERRATA.

Page 6, note [1], for "evangelius," *read* "evangeliis."

Page 13, note [3], for "consepeleri," *read* "consepeliri."

Page 106, note, for "probatus," *read* "probatur."

Page 109, note [3], for "est," *read* "esse."

CORRIGENDA.

Amended translations of a few difficult passages have been communicated to the *Revue Celtique*. The following are worthy of attention:—

Page 22, Rom. viii. 32, for "His coming would not have availed us," *read* "it would not have happened to Him."

Page 41, Rom. xv. 8, for "that He is true God," *read* "that God is true."

Page 45, 1 Cor. i. 14, for "till He came," *read* "till it came by His cross."

Page 62, 1 Cor. xii. 12, for "Christ deems the saints and the just one body," *read* "Christ hath one body, the saints and the just."

Page 81, 2 Cor. xiii. 2, for "read," *insert* "read out."

Page 87, Eph. i. 18, for "clear," *read* "keen."

www.ingramcontent.com/pod-product-compliance
Lightning Source LLC
Chambersburg PA
CBHW030356170426
43202CB00010B/1394